D0307056

# GREATEST
# MISTAKES
# AND
# MYSTERIES

# GREATEST
# MISTAKES
# AND
# MYSTERIES

Catastrophes, disasters and
strange events

**BLITZ EDITIONS**

Published by Blitz Editions
an imprint of Bookmart Ltd
Registered Number 2372865
Trading as Bookmart Ltd
Desford Road
Enderby
Leicester LE9 5AD


ISBN 1 85605 107 2

This material has previously appeared in *Strange But True*


Thanks to the Hulton Picture Company and
Mary Evans Picture Library for sourcing pictures.

50927

# Contents

# Greatest Mistakes and Mysteries

People like comfort and security.
Frightened of uncertainty and petrified of chaos,
we all like to know what is going to happen tomorrow and
the day after that.
But the disturbing truth is that while we live in a world apparently ordered
and reasonable, we continue to
witness events which prove that just under the surface is a minefield of
mysteries, tragedies and the unexpected just waiting to burst upon us.
Outside the small circle of our everyday lives there are questions we cannot
begin to answer,
enigmas we cannot hope to comprehend and
dangers that make our blood run cold.

GREATEST MISTAKES AND MYSTERIES takes us
on a journey through this disturbing landscape - a landscape inhabited by
ghosts and UFOs and strange legends,
by appalling natural disasters and by manmade horrors.
From the sinking of the 'unsinkable' Titanic to
the calamity at the Chernobyl nuclear reactor,
and from shattering earthquakes to strange encounters with unidentified
objects, this book will prove that
a bewildering and terrifying world is closer to
us than we dare to think.

# MISTAKES AND DISASTERS

# THE TITANIC
# Voyage to Disaster

They dined and danced under the glittering chandeliers ... and then they drowned in the icy North Atlantic. A single iceberg had destroyed for ever the myth of the unsinkable Titanic

She was built as the greatest ship of this or any age. Bigger, mightier, stronger, she was named *Titanic*, and she was unsinkable. The RMS *Titanic* went down on her maiden voyage in 1912, with the loss of over 1500 lives. So arrogant were the builders and operators of the gigantic vessel that they proclaimed: 'God himself could not sink this ship.' God didn't have to - all it took was a mammoth iceberg that buckled and ripped the double-steel, compartmented hull, causing the ice cold waters of the North Atlantic to flood in and sink her in just a matter of hours.

As the band played 'Nearer My God to Thee' and the ship slid below the icy, black waters, her passing seemed to mirror that of the golden age before World War I. Tom Shales, a Washington writer, said: 'The ship was not only a ship, but a time capsule, and it could be

*Above: First Officer Wilde who was on the bridge of the White Star liner when it sank beneath the waves with the loss of all but 705 of its 2227 passengers.*

*Opposite: The 46,000-ton Titanic is towed from her berth for sea trials prior to her disastrous maiden voyage in April 1912. She cost £4 million - about £100 million by today's value.*

*Left: Bruce Ismay, managing director of the White Star Line, leaves the Customs House in Southampton.*

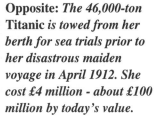

**Right:** *Four towering funnels indicate the astonishing 900-ft length of the ill-fated giant of the high seas. Her height was the equivalent of an eleven-storey building.*

**Below:** *Some of the twenty lifeboats on the* **Titanic.** *Many more lives could have been saved if the liner had been equipped with more of them.*

said she took the glittery, self-indulgent golden age with her to the grave.'

But the simple, inescapable fact of the *Titanic* tragedy is that it need never have happened if the White Star Line, her owners, had equipped her with enough lifeboats. They were left off in the utter belief she could not sink.

The *Titanic* began life as the largest moving object on earth in the drawing offices of the great Harland and Wolff shipyards in Belfast, Northern Ireland; she was conceived at a time when trans-

Atlantic liner traffic was at its peak between Britain and Europe and the New World. It was to be built for luxury and speed, but not for safety.

Nevertheless, the engineers had come up with a 'revolutionary' design which would keep the ship afloat no matter what maritime accident befell it. The design was a series of watertight compartments, sixteen in all, running the length of the hull. The bulkheads separating them were also supposedly stronger and more efficient than those in use on any other ship, naval or merchant.

The makers boasted that up to two compartments could be flooded without the ship listing seriously. Not only the finest engineers, but the finest shipwrights, carpenters, tradesmen and designers were employed to make her the most luxurious vessel afloat. Everything about her was breathtaking and superlative. She was 900 feet long with four funnels, each 22 feet in diameter. From top to bottom she was the height of an eleven-storey building, and she weighed 46,000 tons. The rudder was as tall as a large mansion; the engines could produce 50,000 horsepower to move the ship at 23 knots; and there was enough electricity to power a small town.

For the first-class passengers there was unparalleled luxury. There was the first swimming pool aboard a ship - a great novelty - and a special crane which loaded and unloaded cars so the mobile millionaire could take his luxury limousine with him on a voyage. They could avail themselves of Arabian-style Turkish baths, a gym, a squash court, a lounge modelled after a room at Versailles, a Parisian cafe and a palm court.

There were sumptuous suites and cabins for 735 first-class passengers and cabins for a further 1650 passengers in second and third classes.

---

'The Millionaire's Special' had the first-ever swimming pool on board a ship

---

The White Star Line was proud to hype the *Titanic* as the greatest ship ever. Her passenger list for the maiden voyage from Southampton to New York read like a veritable *Who's Who* of the rich and famous of the day: there was the financier Benjamin Guggenheim, for whom the famous art museum was named in New York in a gesture to his philanthropy; Isador Straus, part owner

of Macy's department store, the American painter Francis Millet and the man who built the Brooklyn Bridge.

The *Titanic* had cost £4 million to construct - equivalent today to £100 million - and she steamed under British and American flags from Southampton on her maiden voyage on 10 April 1912. On her decks were twenty lifeboats - four more than required under British Board of Trade regulations, but still woefully few for the passengers on board. Sixteen lifeboats, it was later calculated, would hold just one quarter of the passengers and crew aboard.

*Survivors from the* Titanic *wait to be recovered from the choppy waters of the icy North Atlantic. Few were as lucky. Those in the water died of extreme cold in two minutes.*

## THE VOYAGE OF DOOM

Five days out at sea, the crew of the *Titanic* reported nothing extraordinary in the bitterly cold weather as the ship ploughed on towards the Grand Banks of Newfoundland. At night on the 14th the sea was glassy calm, but there had been sightings of icebergs in the area. They did not perturb Captain Smith, whose ship sliced through the starry night at 21.5 knots per hour.

Then, in the crow's nest, a lookout suddenly shouted at 11.40pm: 'Iceberg, right ahead!' and accompanied his shout with a warning bell that rang three times. Thirty seconds later the liner and the iceberg met in a collision that jolted the great ship, hurling ice on to the teak decks to the delight of first-class passengers who emerged moments later enthralled by the sight of the chunks of icecap littering them.

They did not know that the collision was, for the majority of them, their death knell. One of the survivors said later: 'So

*Above: American tycoon Isador Straus lost his life in the Titanic disaster. Part owner of Macy's department store, New York, he was just one of ten equally rich passengers aboard the so-called 'Millionaire's Special'.*

*Above right: Isador's wife Ida, who refused the offer of a place in a lifeboat and instead died in her husband's arms aboard the liner.*

the crash came and it sounded like this to me, like tearing a strip off a piece of calico, nothing more ... Later it grew in intensity ... as though someone had drawn a giant finger along the side of the ship.'

---

After the impact, first-class passengers laughed in delight at the shattered chunks of iceberg on the decks

---

The iceberg had risen some 90 feet out of the water and its massive submerged bulk had ripped a huge rent in the starboard section of the vessel, rupturing the watertight compartments in which so much faith had been placed. The behemoth was now taking on water at a phenomenal rate - 16,000 cubic feet of slate grey, cold Atlantic in the first forty minutes alone.

The first five compartments were completely flooded, with water slopping over into compartment 6, then compartment 7, and so on, filling them up one by one until the ship eventually sank.

On the bridge the unthinkable was slowly beginning to come home to Captain Smith, who at first could not believe his ears when his officers told him of the catastrophe taking place below. At almost exactly midnight he ordered the passengers to take to the boats while a message was flashed out that she was sinking.

Many human dramas occurred that have gone into legend; Ida Straus refused the offer of a place in a lifeboat and died in her beloved husband's arms as the liner sank beneath the waves.The chairman of the White Star Line showed no such courage and jumped into a lifeboat, thereafter forever condemned to live a life of disgrace.

Mining tycoon Guggenheim and his valet Victor Giglio dressed in evening clothes and prepared to meet their Maker like gentlemen. Ten millionaires died and valuables, including diamonds valued at £4 million, were consigned to the deep along with their owners.

Confusion reigned on the boat deck, not aided by the fact that the crewmen had never performed a proper boat drill during her sea trials. There were collapsible rafts as well as lifeboats but these were not assembled in time, or were stored in inaccessible places.

As the ship began to list dramatically distress rockets were fired into the darkness, the last faint hopes of a captain

*Below: **How the news was relayed on the streets of London. The 'unsinkable' ship had met an unthinkable fate.***

*Bottom: **Survivors huddle pitifully on makeshift beds. They had been picked up by the** Carpathia **which steamed belatedly to the wreck site.***

grasping for any salvation for his doomed passengers and crew. He didn't think anyone would see them - but people *did* - the crewmen aboard the passenger liner *California*, which was only nineteen miles away.

But due to incredible blunders the crew misread the distress flares as belonging to another vessel and sat in blissful ignorance in the icefield until way after five the next morning, long after the *Titanic* had slipped to her icy grave. It was later learned that the *California*'s skipper assumed that the rockets had been a false alarm.

---

The liner California saw the distress flares but interpreted them as a false alarm

---

The greatest tragedy on board that night befell the 670 immigrants in third class, or steerage, who were trapped below decks in doors kept locked by order of the US Immigration Department. By the time they had battered their way to the outside most of the lifeboats had slipped from their davits.

In two hours and thirty-five minutes the *Titanic* was almost at a 90-degree angle in the water, her lights twinkling and refracting on the water, casting an eerie, phosphorescent glow across the smooth sea.

Five minutes later she went under, creating a huge vortex on the surface that dragged down people and debris with it in a giant whirlpool. There was an agonizing hissing and massive air bubbles as the boilers exploded on the ship's slow descent through 13,000 feet of water.

The *Carpathia* was steaming now towards the wreck site and arrived an hour later to pick up the pitifully few survivors. Two thousand two hundred and twenty-seven people were on board the ship when it left Southampton; just 705 survived.

### THE UNDERSEA GRAVE

For seventy-three years she lay undisturbed in her watery grave, a testimony to man's folly. The *Titanic*

Left: *Shock and horror soon turned to outrage and sympathy...children put money in a collecting box outside London's Mansion House.*

Opposite: *A cross-section of the* Titanic *shows how the iceberg tore through the hull between the foremast and the first funnel.*

Below: *A silent throng watches as the Lord Mayor of London arrives at St Paul's Cathedral for the memorial service to the* Titanic's *victims.*

became a byword for doomed ventures of heroism, cowardice, excitement and adventure. Historical societies were formed, as were survivors' associations and salvage merchants dreamed of raising her and her spoils within.

It was widely assumed that she would still be in one piece on the ocean floor when in July 1986 American oceanographer Dr Robert Ballard led an undersea team which found her. But, in the eerie, cold light, it was seen that she had broken up into three pieces - crushed by the water pressure on her descent.

In a 1600-metre debris field Ballard found the bow section, buckled under its own weight, embedded 600 metres from the stern section. In the middle was the collapsed remains of the *Titanic's* middle.

In the debris field itself are the artefacts of a lost age; an entire kitchen of copper implements, wine bottles with their corks still in them, coffee cups with the emblem of the White Star Line unfaded through the years, bathtubs, bedsprings, toilets, doorknobs, chandeliers, stoves and ceramic dolls heads that were once owned by little children who are now pensioners or long since dead.

One of the most poignant images his high-tech cameras captured was of a broken lifeboat davit, hanging limply on the edge of the ship, a silent testimony to a night that the world will never forget. A night, in fact, to remember.

BILGE KEEL

THE BUCKLED PLATES

FIRST CLASS STATE ROOMS

POST MAIL ROOM

DOUBLE BOTTOM

KEEL

ICE PENETRATING THE DOUBLE BOTTOM

# KUWAIT OILFIELDS
## A Dictator's Revenge

A power-hungry dictator behaving like a latter-day Hitler - but when Saddam Hussein's plans to occupy Kuwait were foiled he revenged himself on the world by unleashing environmental pollution of unimaginable magnitude

I t began as a power-play, a quest for real and imagined respect among the nations of the world who would view him as a modern-day liberator. It ended in total, utter and abject defeat, with 100,000 of his countrymen dead, his nation bombed into pre-industrial bleakness, his factories reduced to ashes and twisted steel.

The Iraqi dictator Saddam Hussein's desert adventure was but a blip in history - an occupation of his neighbour Kuwait that lasted less than six months, followed by an air and ground war of less than six weeks which put paid to his grand vision as the Arab strong man seeking to find a place in the sun for all his people.

But there is no sun now on Iraq's

**Above:** *An Iraqi tank guards the entrance to Kuwait's Sheraton Hotel from where Europeans and Americans were rounded up.*

**Opposite:** *A sea of foul oil washes up on a Persian Gulf beach at the Kuwait-Saudi border. The oil had been released intentionally to hamper Desert Storm operations.*

**Left:** *On the first day of the invasion, 2 August 1990, Iraqi tanks stream into Kuwait City.*

**Above:** *Two oil-soaked cormorants on a Saudi beach near the Kuwaiti border. The birds can barely move, victims of the massive, deliberate slick measuring 8 miles by 30 miles.*

**Above right:** *An American marine surveys the oil-slick damage. He has turned away from a dead cormorant, suffocated by the black tide.*

horizon, or Kuwait's - it is blacked out in the stench and haze of six hundred burning oil wells.

It may be two years or more before the American and British fire-fighting teams have finally conquered each of the blown well-heads. By that time the damage to the planet may be beyond repair.

On the economic front, the Kuwaitis will have seen £100 billion worth of oil go up in smoke, and a further £25 billion worth lost in the desert sands. Nightly, on prime-time TV across the world, viewers have been given a glimpse of hell, where the fires obscure the sun at midday and young children cough their lungs out in the poisoned atmosphere. The orange fireballs roar like some mythical dragon, sending soot falling like snow across the desert wastes, blackening everything in its path.

The rain falls gooey black, mingling with the already polluted waters of the once-pristine Persian Gulf. The smoke-cloud cover makes the desert temperature 20 degrees cooler at midday and, depending on which way the wind blows, can blot out huge chunks of Kuwait City during the rush hours.

### A NUCLEAR WINTER IN PROSPECT

As soon as Saddam's forces fanned out across the oilfields after his invasion of Kuwait in August 1990 the top priority for his sappers and engineers were the oil derricks in Burgan - the second largest oilfield in the world - Wafra, Sabriya, Umm Gudair, Ahmadi, Khasman, Bahra, Rugei, Raudhaitan, Mutriba and Minagish. The Russian explosive charges on the wellheads were proof positive of his plan to make good on his threat of destruction.

---

Darkness at noon was just one sinister result of Saddam's deliberate devastation of the Kuwaiti oilfields

---

Some wells were exploded during the air war - the blame being put on the bombs that were poured down on Iraqi positions by allied warplanes - and the rest were set off at twenty second intervals as the coalition's armoured spearheads smashed through the defences at breakneck speed.

The liberation of Kuwait thus took place under a black sky, in an atmosphere dangerous to breathe.

The well fires are sustained by the huge natural pressure from beneath the desert surface in the oil reservoir, pushing the oil to the surface at speeds of one thousand miles per hour.

Five hundred thousand tons of oil-related pollutants are spewed out daily by the oil well fires - ten times the amount emitted by all American industrial and power-generating plants combined. Toxic chemicals, including hydrogen sulphide, sulphur dioxide, carbon monoxide and hydrocarbons, are among the deadly particles trapped in the black, oily smoke.

## HUMAN AND ECOLOGICAL VICTIMS

The smoke may yet trigger one of the deadliest scenarios in the environmental lexicon - a nuclear winter where the smoke rises into the atmosphere to cut off sunlight and air, turning parts of the earth into permafrost zones.

**Above:** *As allied forces continued to advance on Kuwait City in February 1991, Iraqi prisoners were led away from the desert in their thousands.*

**Below:** *Smoke and flames from burning Kuwaiti oil wells were visible for scores of miles around.*

At ground level, the burning oil wells threaten the delicate ecosystem of the desert itself. Although a desert may seem a lifeless place, it is in fact home to myriad species of insects, scorpions and snakes as well as to larger animals such as camels and gazelles. Micro-organisms form a crust on the desert floor in much the same way as coral forms under the sea. This crust catches the seeds of shrubs and prevents the sand from blowing away.

Now over 300 square miles of desert lies under oil - some of it inches deep, others vast lakes six feet and more in depth - the result of spewing gushers that did not ignite when the retreating Iraqis blew the wellheads.

It will be decades before the full ecological effects of these oil lakes can be evaluated, but in the short term they spell catastrophe for the desert's fragile infrastructure. Where the surface has not been flooded by oil it has been turned into sheets of glass, the result of searing 4000 degree temperatures.

The first victims of the smoke are people with respiratory problems. Asthma and bronchitis sufferers are already queuing up for aid in Kuwait and as far away as Bahrain, where the smog drifts when the wind blows in the wrong direction.

But far more worrying are the fears

about future generations. Because of the high volume of cancer-causing agents trapped in the smoke, doctors say babies could be born deformed, in much the same way that the escape of radiation at the Chernobyl power plant in the Soviet Union has triggered an appalling number of mutations in both human beings and animals.

### FIGHTING THE FIRES

But that is a problem for the future. Currently firefighters from Texas, Britain and Belgium are battling the blazes at what seems at times like an agonizingly slow pace. Wearing nothing more hi-tech than cotton overalls, the £600 per day firefighters are slowly dousing the wells, using a combination of guts, brute force and wily know-how gleaned from tackling oil fires around the globe.

Under a constant barrage of water, they move towards the intense heat of the flames in cranes shielded with tin sheeting. Using either dynamite to blow out the flames or specially moulded steel to snuff them out, they then move in with a new set of valves called a Christmas Tree which they fit on to the pipe and gradually close to form a seal. One mistake and they will be blown sky-high.

**Above:** *Workmen dug fresh graves in Kuwait City's Raqqua cemetery as victims caught up in the fighting were discovered.*

**Right:** *The picture that told the world that the Gulf War was over. Thousands of Iraqi vehicles - private and military - had been blasted by allied forces.*

Red Adair, the Texan oil firefighter who bravely led his men against the inferno on the Piper Alpha oil rig disaster in the North Sea which claimed over a hundred lives, is awed by the spectacle of the burning wellheads. He said:

*Each one in its own right would be a disaster. And we have hundreds of them to deal with. We have to improvise every step of the way - there is nothing cast in stone about how each one must be tackled. People who say we are not working fast enough don't know the power that we are dealing with. The job is as tough as hell and we are working seven days a week.*

Even so, it could be two years before the fires are extinguished and the wellheads capped.

## MARINE POLLUTION

No less of an environmental disaster has been created by Saddam and his forces in the Persian Gulf - again the target of the Iraqi dictator's unique brand of eco-terrorism. More than 460 million gallons of unrefined crude oil were leaked into the waters that are home to thousands of fish and seabirds and were once rich fishing grounds harvested by Arabs from several nations. Shrimp beds have been decimated, and the breeding grounds of rare marine life lost forever. The damage is truly incalculable.

The slick is still there, months after the end of the war. Thousands of seabirds and fish have died, the TV images of their bloated, pathetic bodies bobbing on oil-thick waves evoking more sympathy in Western nations than did the Iraqi dead on the road to Basra at the war's end.

Millions of gallons of oil have been skimmed from the Gulf already, but millions more have washed ashore to bake in the hot climate, forming a permanent tar pavement over beaches.

An estimated twenty thousand or more seabirds have died so far. The spring months are the worst, as forty-five different species of birds use the Gulf as a refuelling spot on the northward migration from Africa and Arabia to their summer breeding grounds in northern Europe, the sub-Arctic and beyond. Many of these sandpipers, plovers, redshanks and others will die in the fouled waters for years to come. One or two, like the red-necked phalarope, might even be lost altogether to their native breeding grounds.

## A BLEAK FUTURE?

Dr Hassan Nasrallah, a climatologist, warns that the final consequences of the environmental disaster in Kuwait may not be understood for decades. He said:

*We are talking about massive sources of pollution of a kind that have never been monitored before. The world has no experience of a conflagration of the kind which has engulfed Kuwait. Humankind has done this awful thing to the planet and humankind will have to see what permanent damage has been done.*

**Below:** *Long after the fighting was over, the oil fields of Kuwait continued to burn, lighting up the skies and polluting the entire region.*

# THE HINDENBURG
## Flames in the Sky

The airship Hindenburg was built in the thirties as a symbol of Hitler's new Germany, and her safety procedures were second to none. So why did she explode in a blazing inferno in May 1937?

The *Hindenburg* was by far the most luxurious airship of all time, a floating palace dedicated to comfort, grandeur and efficiency as she ferried her wealthy clientele across the Atlantic.

She was so vast and so graceful, that she was to aviation what the once-mighty *Titanic* had been to shipping. And ironically, like the great liner which had sunk below the icy waters of the Atlantic Ocean twenty-five years earlier, the *Hindenburg*, too, was destined for disaster.

As she approached her dock at the Lakehurst naval station in New Jersey in May 1937, the great airship exploded into a fiery ball. Flames swept through the 198,000 cubic metres of highly inflammable hydrogen which filled the belly of the craft. In a scant thirty-two seconds the *Hindenburg*, more than twice the length of a football field, had been reduced to a charred skeleton of twisted metal. And in her death throes she had taken thirty-six people with her.

What happened? Was it an act of God, or was it sabotage? Even today, over half a century later, the answer remains as much a riddle as it did then.

### HITLER'S FLAGSHIP

The tragic events of 6 May 1937 came just two years after the *Hindenburg* was completed, and less than twelve months after her first test flight. Symbolizing the

**Above:** *The promenade deck of the* **Hindenburg,** *literally the last word in air travel luxury in the 1930s.*

**Opposite:** *The huge bulk of the new airship fills its hangar. Her proud builders regarded her as the safest means of flight in the world.*

**Below:** *She was to the skies what the* **Titanic** *had been to the high seas. Both behemoths, however, were equally ill-fated.*

**Above:** *Proudly marked with the Nazis' swastika emblem, the tail of Hitler's flagship, the* **Hindenburg** *protrudes from its hangar.*

rise of the Third Reich, she was considered a national treasure, the largest, most expensive dirigible ever made. To the Fuehrer, Adolf Hitler, she was incontrovertible proof of the Aryan supremacy he so often bragged about.

To her builders, however, she was more than a showpiece of Nazi Germany. She was also the safest means of flight, fitted out with the most advanced security measures then available.

---

Regulations obliged both crew and passengers to hand over their matches and lighters before boarding

---

Indeed, safety measures were even more stringent than on other vessels. The crew wore anti-static overalls and shoes soled with hemp, and all those aboard - including passengers - had to hand over

their matches and lighters before they were allowed to board.

The airship's safety mechanisms were matched only by the grandeur of her many facilities, including quiet, comfortable state rooms.

The bar served the speciality of the ship, the LZ-129 Frosted Cocktail - gin with a dash of orange juice that took its name from the formal designation of the *Hindenburg*.

The meals were prepared by the finest chefs that Germany had to offer, and served on blue and gold porcelain. There was even a specially constructed, lightweight piano aboard for entertainment.

Most of the pampered passengers, however, preferred to spend their time relaxing in the observation room or cupola - a room enclosed by windows and attached to the craft's underbelly.

have been taken hold by a number of men in the field. The back motors of the ship are holding it just enough to keep it... it's burst into flame! This is terrible! The flames are 500 feet into the sky...

Then, choking back tears, he forced himself to continue: 'This is the worst thing I've ever witnessed. It is one of the worst catastrophes in the world. Oh, the humanity! All the passengers! I don't believe it!'

'It's a terrible crash,' he concluded. 'It's just lying there, a massive smoking

### 'A MASSIVE SMOKING WRECK'

Everything seemed to be going smoothly on 6 May 1937, as the giant craft passed so low over the Manhattan skyline that passengers waving from open windows in her vast silver belly came almost face to face with news photographers perched atop the Empire State Building.

But as the *Hindenburg* neared the Lakehurst naval station several hours late, after being buffeted by high winds on her eleventh transatlantic crossing, tragedy struck. Just seconds after her guide-ropes had been lowered for mooring and eventual landing, she exploded into a towering inferno above the stunned crowd which had gathered to greet the giant airship. The explosion was so loud that it could be heard fifteen miles away.

---

**As the hydrogen in the Hindenburg's belly ignited, the explosion was heard fifteen miles away**

---

Well-known radio reporter Herbert Morrison, on hand to describe the *Hindenburg's* arrival in a broadcast to the American people, gave what is still considered to be the definitive description of the disaster.

As the huge airship neared, he began his report:

*The ropes have been dropped and they*

**Above:** *The* Hindenburg *was the largest - and most expensive - dirigible ever made.*

**Right:** *Forget sea travel ... this was the new way to span the globe in the optimistic Thirties.*

**Below right:** *The* Hindenburg *was a 'hotel' in the sky, with every comfort of a luxury liner.*

wreck.' Before their eyes, and those of other horrified witnesses, the *Hindenburg* was quickly consumed by the inferno, which fed itself on the vast hydrogen bags kept in its belly. Panicked passengers and crew jumped from the windows and doors to the ground below in a mad dash to escape the flames as the airship lurched and thrashed. The smell of burning flesh and the screams of the dying filled the night air. Meanwhile, as pandemonium was erupting all about him, Commander Max Pruss, a seasoned Zeppelin pilot, did his best to right the ship. He did not abandon the vessel until it crashed to the ground. Miraculously, Pruss and sixty-one other passengers and crew survived the disaster.

### WHAT WENT WRONG?

What had turned the safest means of transportation yet known into a death trap? As reporters and concerned citizens scrambled for an answer, an official board of inquiry was set up to probe the disaster and try to pinpoint the cause of the fire.

At first the commission focused on the possibility of sabotage - not unlikely given the *Hindenburg*'s status as a showpiece of the hated Third Reich. Once sabotage had been ruled out, the commission considered numerous other possible causes, including leaking gas valves, static electricity and engine sparks. But nothing proved definitive.

Despite the outcry, however, the file on the *Hindenburg* disaster was closed. It would remain so until eight years later, after the end of World War II, when it finally emerged that the Nazis had wielded a strong influence over the official inquiry.

In fact, it become known that Hermann Goering, head of the Luftwaffe and once heir apparent to Hitler, had actually ordered the commission not to investigate the possibility of sabotage too thoroughly. The destruction of a Nazi symbol was embarrassment enough. Aryan pride could not take another blow by admitting that a saboteur had been responsible.

That possibility was raised again some thirty-five years later, when Michael

**Right:** *As it approached its mooring at Lakehurst naval station, an explosion of flames began to engulf the* **Hindenburg.**

**Below:** *'This is terrible,' announced radio commentator Herbert Morrison. 'The flames are 500 feet into the sky.'*

MacDonald Mooney claimed in his book that the disaster was no accident, but planned destruction by a young anti-Nazi saboteur. He identified the perpetrator as Erich Spehl, a twenty-five-year-old blond, blue-eyed airship rigger from the Black Forest, who perished in the flames.

He also alleged that both German and American officials agreed to the cover-up because they did not want to spark 'an international incident'. Although it can never be proved for certain that the *Hindenburg* was sabotaged and that Spehl was the misguided culprit, one thing can be stated beyond a doubt. The tragedy was the finale of an era when luxury was prized as greatly as speed.

Immediately after the crash, Germany halted all commercial Zeppelin services.

The *Hindenburg*'s sister ship, the LZ-130 or *Graf Zeppelin II*, was none the less completed - but Hitler's new-found antagonism towards airships soon led to the scrapping of all Zeppelins and ended the airship programme.

Eventually the *Graf Zeppelin II* was used to carry out spying missions against Britain. Interestingly, the *Hindenburg*, too, became part of the German war effort. The wreckage of the once-proud airship, which had peacefully plied the skies in quiet serenity, was shipped back to Germany - and recycled into war planes.

**Below:** *The **Hindenburg's** burnt-out remains. Miraculously 62 passengers and crew survived; 36 people perished.*

# SEVESO
# Cloud of Death

In July 1976 the little Italian town of Seveso was the victim of a terrible accident at the local chemical plant. A deadly cloud of poison gas was discharged into the atmosphere, and its effects may last for generations

**Right:** *Frightened, bewildered, the people of Seveso were evacuated after their town was contaminated in July 1976.*

**Opposite:** *Masked specialists worked day and night in an almost futile attempt to clean up the chemical plant.*

**Below:** *Animals and plants over many square miles were affected when a safety valve burst at the Seveso chemical factory...which then billowed out its poisonous cloud.*

For years after 'it' happened, the ghost town of Seveso in Northern Italy still idled like some gigantic science-fiction movie set, shuttered behind a Berlin Wall of environmental quarantine panels. 'CONTAMINATED AREA - NO ADMITTANCE' read notices in five languages. Across the top of the panels and into the scarred area hung limp telephone cables attached to the sides of the humble houses within.

But the phones did not ring any more, for there was no one to answer them. The core of Seveso was a dead zone, snuffed out in one of mankind's worst chemical accidents. It would become known as the Italian Hiroshima.

It happened on 10 July 1976, when an explosion at the Swiss-owned Icmesa

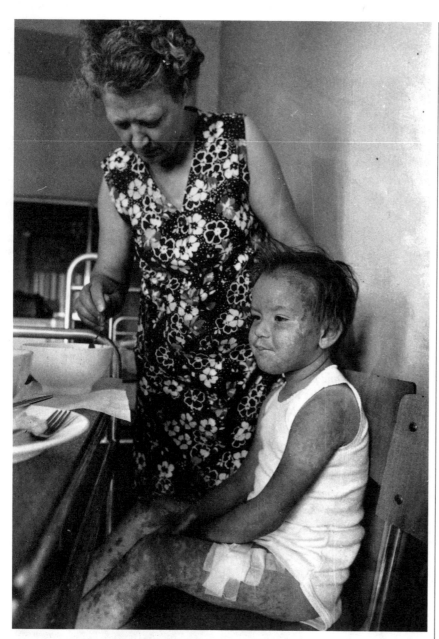

Above: *Little Alice Senno, aged four, was one of the many young victims of the poison gas cloud that escaped from the chemical plant near her home.*

supply of a major city would be enough to wipe out 8 million people; on that black summer day there was enough released in its concentrated form to wipe out 100 million. The long term effects upon the blighted land and the unborn babies of future generations have still to be assessed.

### A STRANGE WHISTLING NOISE

The seventeen thousand residents of Seveso, a town nestling in the green foothills of the Po valley, still had plenty of countryside around them to offset the sprawling factories which fanned out from Milan.

At the plant, which employed many local people, Viro Romani, a technician, was just finishing his lunch. Since it was a Saturday there was no active production going on at the works, so only ten of the 160 employees were on duty.

The firm, a subsidiary of the massive Hoffman-La Roche pharmaceutical companies - one of the world's largest - used the trichlorophenol, or TCP, for the manufacture of hexachlorophene, the active ingredient in many soaps. Hexachlorophene had been banned in the USA but was still widely used in a number of other nations.

The plant's chemical reactor was closed that day, but as Viro Romani sipped his coffee in the canteen there was a loud bang followed by an eerie, piercing whistling. The men ran outside in time to witness the escape of the lethal dioxin, which spewed out at tremendous pressure from the safety valves on top of the apparatus.

---

Families preparing lunch were suddenly seized by fits of coughing as the cloud rolled over them

---

chemical plant discharged a thick white cloud of dioxin, one of the deadliest poisons known to man, over about six square miles of the small industrial suburb some thirteen miles from Milan. As the poison settled on homes and gardens in the following days thousands of pets died, crops were infected and hundreds of people developed nausea, blurred vision and a disfiguring disease known as chloracne.

As at Chernobyl, which came after it, human error unleashed on the unsuspecting innocents of Seveso a man-made disaster of epic proportions.

Dioxin is a by-product of trichlorophenol, used in germicides, deodorants and soaps. Four ounces in the water

Within minutes fine particles of the chemical were falling like snow while the air filled with the pungent smell of chlorine. As emergency taps were turned on to pour cold water inside the reactor the cloud rolled away gently over the Italian countryside on its ominous journey. Families sitting at cafes in the streets or making lunch in their homes

**Left:** *Notices were hastily erected to 'quarantine' the area around Seveso. They remained in place for years afterwards.*

**Below:** *Italian soldiers erect barbed wire fencing around the polluted area of Seveso. Meanwhile hundreds of people were bundled on to evacuation buses.*

were suddenly stricken with fits of coughing and tears rolled down their cheeks. Later in the day, when the cloud had moved on, they complained of headaches and nausea, and a lingering, acrid smell like burned plastic hanging in the air.

### WHY DID IT HAPPEN?

During the first twenty-four hours after the explosion the officials of the plant began their inquest into what had gone wrong. It seemed that the heat of the chemical reaction from the previous day's production had not cooled properly.

To deal with this potential problem, most companies have safety valves like the ones installed at the Seveso plant, and back them up with enormous dump tanks ready to absorb lethal poisons before they can be discharged into the atmosphere. But Seveso had no such dump tanks, and the safety valve not only failed at the crucial moment, but was located on the vent pipe leading to the roof. The result was the escape of the gas.

### IMMEDIATE EFFECTS

It was only after the first three or four days that the full impact of what had happened began to hit home. By Wednesday the doctors' surgeries in Seveso were crammed with people - many of them children - suffering an abundance of ugly rashes and weeping boils, complaining of backache, sickness and blinding headaches.

Patients told the doctors that animals and birds in their gardens and vegetable plots had been dying suddenly. An old man saw three robins on his grass just keel over and die, as if the will to live had gone. Cats and dogs would walk down the street and drop dead. Tomato plants and maize fields seemed burned, the vegetation dry and crumbling, while in the pastures the stricken cattle began bleeding from their eyes and ears. Entire chicken roosts were destroyed, the pathetic carcasses rotting in the summer heat.

Doctors began to grow angry at the lack of information from factory bosses. News about it travelled slowly. There had been no huge explosion, no fire, to warrant the accident reaching the prime-time news broadcasts, so the company stayed silent.

It was on Friday, when a two-year-old baby was rushed into the local hospital, a mass of blisters and rashes, that the mayors of Seveso and nearby Meda pressed Icmesa officials for some answers. The company bosses worriedly said that the soil samples were being examined by boffins in Switzerland, but admitted that posters and warning notices about not eating local produce should be posted around town.

Overnight another eighteen children

were taken to hospital and by now a state approaching panic was beginning to grip the innocent citizens of Seveso.

Birds were now no longer dropping in ones or twos from the sky, but in whole flocks. The animals seemed to be suffering more quickly than the humans, probably because they ate grass, drank rainwater and were generally closer to the fall-out of dioxin than were people. But the doctors, relying on information supplied by the company, were treating the patients as if they had been exposed to TCP - a mild irritant and a million times less toxic than dioxin.

## THE TRUTH DISCOVERED

Bruno Ambrosi, a newsman working in Milan, had a university knowledge of chemistry and found out that dioxin was manufactured in TCP when the temperature of the chemical goes over 200 degrees.

That, he discovered chillingly, is exactly what had happened.

One paper he read about it said: 'It is the most potent small-molecule toxin known to man. Its effects dwarf those of arsenic and strychnine.' Dioxin attacked the liver and kidneys and it was also 'mutagenic' - it had the power to change the chromosomes in the body, leading to cancer and to birth defects in unborn children.

Ambrosi broke the story just as the Swiss scientists confirmed what he already knew to be true - that massive amounts of dioxin had escaped and leached into the soil and atmosphere, with catastrophic effects. Dioxin was insoluble in water, and once it penetrated a substance it could stay there for years.

## STATE OF EMERGENCY

An emergency centre was set up in an elementary school, and local health workers were drafted in to run it. Eight days after the accident the Italian government declared a state of emergency.

Vittoria Rivolta, health minister in the province of Lombardy, began correlating the data on a huge map to try to chart where the cloud had gone and so

**Below:** *An Italian carabiniere feeds a cow. But like thousands of other farm creatures contaminated by the escaping poison, it had to be destroyed later.*

years thousands of tons of soil were removed and buried in concrete, while thousands of tons of plants and seventy thousand animal corpses were burned. Refugees were relocated in temporary accommodation, compensated for loss of produce and property, and promised new housing equal to that which they had abandoned.

Most of the 736 families evacuated were eventually returned to their homes, but 256 people were permanently locked out of the exclusion area in Zone A, where dioxin levels were the highest. An official report three years later by the Italian parliament damned the operators of the chemical plant. It said the plant was unsafe to begin with, and revealed that company officials waited twenty-seven hours after the accident before notifying even the most minor municipal official. The company went on to pay some £8 million pounds in compensation.

Miraculously, no humans have yet died. Some babies have been born with mutated insides, but it is not yet clear whether they have been the victims of dioxin. All but two of the 187 children stricken with chloracne recovered.

determine how far the dioxin had spread. On Saturday, 24 July there was a total evacuation from Zone A in the town, an area on Rivolta's map that suffered the most sickness among humans and the most deaths among animals. Two hundred families left the area, which was then cordoned off by police and caribinieri with six miles of barbed wire. Then the men, wearing protective suits, moved through the area killing every creature still left alive in it. At the end of the killing over fifty thousand animals had been slaughtered. There were a further ten thousand corpses from the effects of the dioxin poisoning.

### FEARS FOR THE FUTURE

Dr Anne Walker, a dermatologist who had treated workers in previous dioxin accidents, said the full effects of the tragedy might not show up for two decades. Fear and uncertainty spread among the population.

As thousands upon thousands of tests were carried out on the local people, and they were graded into high-risk, middle-risk and low-risk categories, the Italian government authorized abortions in the region for fear of abnormal births adding to the disaster. Over a period of two

**Above: *The disastrous effects of the poison cloud can clearly be seen on these leaves. The chemical had previously been used as a defoliant in Vietnam.***

**Right: *Animals were generally affected more quickly than humans. Dogs and cats were collected in dustbin liners, as were birds which had fallen from the sky.***

# CHERNOBYL
# Nuclear Nightmare

## Massive radiation readings in Sweden. Then days of Soviet silence about what had really happened. This was the worst disaster the nuclear power industry has ever known - Chernobyl

The first indication that something had gone wrong - terribly, irredeemably wrong - occurred at 9am on Monday, 28 April 1986, as boffins at the Forsmark nuclear power station, sixty miles from the Swedish capital of Stockholm, noticed disturbing signals bleeping on their ghost-green screens.

The signals were measures of radiation, and the horrified scientists feared a massive reactor leak at the power plant entrusted to their high-tech care. A careful and methodical check of all equipment and its monitoring gauges showed no leakage - and yet the sensors indicated that the air they were breathing was four times the ordained safe limit.

Geiger counters were hurriedly deployed for swift checks on all six hundred workers. The readings were haywire, showing that virtually every worker had been exposed to radiation way above safe limits.

Outside it was the same story - samples taken from soil and plant life showed extraordinarily high deposits of radioactive material. Sweden and much of Europe was being infected by a silent, unseen, unscented killer.

Sixty-seven-and-a-half hours earlier Lieutenant-Colonel Leonid Telyatnikov had been enjoying a few well-earned days off when the telephone rang at his home seventy-five miles outside Kiev in the Soviet Ukraine at 1.32am on 26 April. A breathless voice informed him that there had been an 'incident' at the Chernobyl nuclear power plant eighty miles from Kiev.

It was a bright, starlit night as Telyatnikov, leading his crew of twenty-eight firefighters, raced to the scene. A bright orange glow soon appeared on the horizon. 'I had no idea what had happened or what we were heading into,' recalled Telyatnikov. 'But as I approached the plant I could see debris on fire all around like sparklers.

'Then I noticed a bluish glow above the wreckage of reactor four and pockets of fire on surrounding buildings. It was absolutely silent and eerie.' Protected by no more than wellington boots and a hard hat, Telyatnikov, later honoured as a Hero of the Soviet Union, was confronting the worst disaster in thirty-two years of commercial nuclear power's history.

### A WHOLE CONTINENT OF VICTIMS

The partial meltdown of the Chernobyl nuclear reactor caused a tragedy that continues to bring death, suffering and misery to this day. Untold thousands have died from tumours and cancer caused by the explosion. Human beings, cattle and other livestock, have given birth to nightmarish offspring, deformed and mutated by the effects of the radiation. The earth has been scarred forever, and

**Opposite:** *In the early hours of 26 April 1986, it became apparent that a dreadful disaster had occurred at the Chernobyl nuclear power plant near Kiev.*

**Below:** *By the time scientists had arrived to examine the damage, a cloud of nuclear poison was already drifting westwards towards Sweden.*

mankind left to ponder whether the benefits of nuclear energy are not outweighed by the spectre of such a disaster ever occurring again.

By the time the Forsmark scientists had discovered the presence of massive amounts of radiation in the atmosphere, strong winds were carrying it all over Europe. Light rain fell on the salt marshes of Brittany, making the milk in cows' udders toxic. Heavier rain poured down on to the Welsh hillsides, making the tender lamb forbidden flesh. Snow in Finland, Sweden and West Germany was infected too.

The Swedish scientists informed their government that they believed the source for this nuclear volcano, spewing its lethal residue into the skies, was the Soviet Union. But Communist Russia remained silent.

It was not until 9pm Moscow time that night when the Kremlin finally admitted that something had happened - but it gave no indication of the gravity of the mishap. A terse four-sentence statement was read on the evening news in Moscow.

Almost grudging in its admission, the statement said: 'An accident has taken place at the Chernobyl power station and one of the reactors was damaged. Measures are being taken to eliminate the consequences of the accident. Those affected by it are being given assistance. A government commission has been set up.' The announcer then picked up another sheet of paper and went on to read a story about a Soviet peace fund.

---

Moscow's first official announcement was a cover-up - a four-line statement on the nightly news

---

Western governments began to exert diplomatic pressure on the Soviet Union for details of exactly what had happened. But only men like Telyatnikov knew in those first few hours the enormity of the disaster. 'I realized it was not an ordinary situation as soon as I passed through the gate,' he said. 'There was just the noise of machines and the fire crackling. The firefighters knew what they had to do and proceeded quietly, on the run. The

**Above: *Workers go about their duties in a reactor room of the Chernobyl plant. This picture was taken in 1982, four years before the disaster.***

radiation-measuring meters had frozen on their highest level. Thoughts of my family would flash through my mind and be gone. No one would discuss the radiation risk. The most frightening thought was that we wouldn't have enough strength to hold out until reserves came. About an hour after the fire began a group of fire-fighters with symptoms of radiation exposure were taken down from a rooftop close to the damaged reactor. When I approached five men to take up the position they rushed to the rooftop almost before I could get the words out of my mouth. They are all dead now, from radioactive poisoning.'

Telyatnikov too is one of what the

Ukrainians call 'the living dead'. He began vomiting even as he fought the flames and since then has battled cancer, like thousands of others.

The burning white-hot graphite core of the reactor blazed at 5000 degrees Fahrenheit - twice the temperature of molten steel - and thrust millions of cubic feet of radioactive gas into the atmosphere. Pictures taken by a CIA satellite four hundred miles above the earth were on President Ronald Reagan's desk forty-eight hours after the red alert was sounded by the Forsmark scientists. They showed a picture of hell that the embarrassed, technologically inept Soviets, refused to admit publicly.

In the immediate hours after the tragedy Per Olof Sjostedt, technical and scientific adviser at the Swedish embassy in Moscow, contacted officials of the Soviet nuclear energy programme armed with the information given to him via the Forsmark scientists. He was curtly told that there was no information to be had.

It took rising Soviet politician Boris Yeltsin to step forward several days later to lend gravity to his government's so far casual response to the disaster. He said: 'It is serious. Very serious. The cause apparently lies in human error. We are undertaking measures to make sure this doesn't happen again.'

The whole area within an eighteen-mile radius of Chernobyl was evacuated and declared an unfit zone, where cattle, drinking water and vegetation were all deemed unfit for consumption.

## MELTDOWN

Nuclear physicists began to theorize about what had happened at the Chernobyl reactor and came up with a likely scenario. The reactor used uranium fuel rods to generate heat used to boil water into steam. The steam in turn powered turbine generators for power. Cooling water is essential in such a system to stop the fuel rods from super-heating, causing a meltdown or burn-up, in which the core virtually turns itself into a nuclear bomb.

It seems that the water circulation system to provide the cooling liquid had failed, causing the temperature in the reactor core to hit 5000 degrees. The uranium fuel rods melted and produced radioactive steam that reacted with the zirconium alloy cladding of the rods to produce explosive hydrogen gas.

Soviet officials proved reluctant to seek outside assistance while still trying to pretend that not much had happened. But a Soviet scientific officer attached to their embassy in Bonn did approach the West German nuclear power industry with a request for information on fighting graphite core fires. A similar request went out the same day to Swedish authorities, and Moscow invited Californian bone marrow expert Dr Robert Gale to provide medical aid to Chernobyl victims.

---

'Please tell the world to help us!' cried an anguished Russian voice picked up by a Dutch radio ham

---

Moscow tackled the blaze with an army of workers and soldiers - most of them now dead or suffering from the effects of prolonged exposure to such massive dosages of radiation. Helicopters carrying tons of wet sand and

**Below:** *Three months after the blast, clean-up crews hang chunks of graphite from a burnt-out nuclear reactor. Their 'protective' clothing failed to save many of them from cancer and death.*

lead flew over the site and dumped their loads directly on to the blazing reactor. Tons of the element boron, which absorbs neutrons, was also dumped on to the smouldering fires.

### THE TERRIBLE AFTERMATH

By the end of the week the fire was out - but so was the radiation, incalculable amounts of it, spreading an ominous pall over Europe and the western half of the Soviet Union. On the ground, near to the site, the victims began dying of haemorrhages and brain seizures. They were often the lucky ones - the lingering deaths, the mutated stillborn babies, the cancer which racks heroes like fireman Telyatnikov, were yet to come.

In a bid to clean up some of the debris the Soviets dug a huge pit and filled it with shattered remnants of the reactor, twisted metal and broken concrete from the plant and clothes worn by disaster workers. Some 2 million cubic feet of concrete was mixed over the next six weeks and poured on to the reactor, sealing it forever.

As the rescuers struggled, President Reagan became angrier with Moscow, and said so in a nationwide radio address. He told America in his usual Saturday speech: 'The Soviets owe the world an explanation. A full accounting of what happened at Chernobyl and what is happening now is the least the world community has a right to expect.'

Nuclear experts declared the RBMK-1000 reactors at Chernobyl mighty but outdated machines. But most glaringly, said the experts, the Russians showed a distinct lack of care about safety by not building the reactor with a concrete outer structure that could have contained most of the fire and the subsequent radiation.

---

### Ten times as much radiation escaped as at Hiroshima and Nagasaki

---

It is now known that over a hundred thousand people were evacuated from the region. Even the government newspaper *Izvestia* has admitted that as many as 3 million people are still living on irradiated land, selling as well as devouring their produce. After four years of bureaucratic book-cooking, health statistics show an increase in blood disorders, freak offspring and deformed plant life that is unlike anything else found on earth.

Dr Gale, who provided much of the medical expertise the Russians needed for bone marrow transplants on victims, predicts as many as 150,000 new cancer cases in the next ten years as a direct result of the Chernobyl fall-out. In Minsk alone the incidences of leukaemia have doubled in five years.

Due to the outdated technology and stagnant economy of the country, just a fraction of this number will be cured.

### FEAR AND MISTRUST

Chernobyl's most lasting legacy will be the mistrust felt by the country's own citizens about a workers' paradise that condemned people to die with dis-information and disorganization.

---

### Crude technology and disregard for safety were held to blame

---

As to blame for the tragedy, the Soviets were quick to find scapegoats. The former director of the plant, Viktor Bryukhanov, and the former chief engineer, Anatoly Dyatlov, in charge of doomed reactor number four, were both asleep when the cooling system failed and the reactor blew up at 1.23am. They were consequently jailed for dereliction of duty. Two others received three-year prison terms, and two more suspended sentences.

### SICK IRONY

As a macabre postscript to the tragedy of Chernobyl, the Kiev authorities are offering to take death-wish tourists on a tour of the devastated nuclear power plant. Ever hungry for hard currency, the local tourist bureau apparatchiks are hoping to lure Westerners to the dead zone with advertising that promises fairground-type thrills:

*CHILL to the eerie dead city of Chernobyl as you walk through deserted

schools, farms and factories!

*GASP in awe at the tomb of the great melted reactor, now encased in tons of concrete!

*SWOON at the sight of the mutated farm animals born with horrifying defects as a result of the fall-out!

And as if to prove their social responsibility, the organizers behind this macabre voyeurism promise takers of the tour a full medical examination afterwards to check for radiation poisoning. Part of the tour - that will cost up to £200 for a single day - includes visits to the farms and homes where comrades have defied the Kremlin and returned to the land after the explosion.

It is highly unlikely that the land and buildings are completely free from radioactivity.

Some scientists believe that it could be up to a hundred years before the radiation levels have dropped sufficiently for it not to pose a potential health threat. Thirty-seven died in the reactor explosion and

fire. But thousands more have died from radiation poisoning and cancers triggered by the fall-out. Scientist Dr David Abrahamovitz said: 'If tourists were to go there, say, after a rainfall, there would be more chance of a higher radiation level registering than if they went when it was dry because the water would release more toxins in the dry earth. It is not a visit that I would be queuing up to go on.'

Excursion officials say they will also take in the little town of Slavutich, a radiation workers' colony that is home to the people who monitor the dead zone and ensure that the radioactive pile is not leaking from its concrete tomb. The motto of the town is: 'Life is good - but too short!'

American writer Francis Clines said: 'The notion has the virtue of dark candour, of daring to think the outside world might like to at least leer, if not memorialize, an historic outrage upon one of the earth's humbler landscapes.'

**Above:** *It took years for the full horror of the Chernobyl disaster to be revealed. 'The problems will unfold well into the next century,' says Soviet scientist Igor Ignatchev.*

# ZEEBRUGGE FERRY
## Tragedy in the Channel

A short ferry crossing on a familiar stretch of water became a night of hell for crew and passengers. In March 1987 the Herald of Free Enterprise sank as she left port

**Right:** *As dawn broke over the Belgian port of Zeebrugge, the full scale of the tragedy of 6 March 1987 became apparent.*

**Opposite:** *The* **Herald of Free Enterprise** *set sail from Zeebrugge with her bow doors open. It was a recipe for an unparalleled tragedy in maritime history.*

The English Channel is the world's busiest waterway. Each day the narrow sea lane separating Britain from continental Europe is negotiated by thousands of vessels of all shapes, sizes and nationalities. For holidaymakers the ferries which ply between the British, French, Belgian and Dutch ports are regarded as little more than lumbering omnibuses, making the journey with such regularity and such apparent ease that it is often forgotten that the Channel is the graveyard of countless ships, lost in waters that are dangerous and cold.

Weather has undoubtedly played a great part in claiming the lives of stricken vessels. But so too has human error. And it was an appalling chain of human errors - what an official inquiry would later brand forever as 'the disease of sloppiness' - which struck the *Herald of*

*Free Enterprise* as she steamed for Dover from the Belgian port of Zeebrugge on 6 March 1987.

Due to that 'disease of sloppiness', the bow doors of the Townsend Thoresen car ferry were left open as she steamed into the night. Water poured in, unstoppably, flooding the car decks before tilting the ship to a list that was irreversible. She rolled on to her side, saved from sinking only by a shallow sandbank, and in the confusion and chaos that followed 193 people lost their lives.

The agony of that night has been played over and over again in the minds of those who survived, those who were the rescuers, those who saw it on TV, and those who were left to judge the men who caused it.

### 'IT'S DEFINITELY GOING OVER'

The *Herald of Free Enterprise* was a 7951-ton ferry, 132 metres long and part of the Blue Riband fleet operated by Townsend which crossed the Channel in record times. Time, it was later to be learned, was a critical operating factor with Townsend bosses. On the highly competitive Channel routes, turnaround and speed at sea were of the essence if Townsend was to stay ahead of rival shipping lines.

When she steamed out of Zeebrugge that night Captain David Lewry was at the helm. An experienced skipper and a long-time employee of Townsend Thoresen, Captain Lewry was on the

**Below:** *Passengers had no time to don lifejackets as the ferry rolled on its side, hurling them into the freezing waters in pitch darkness.*

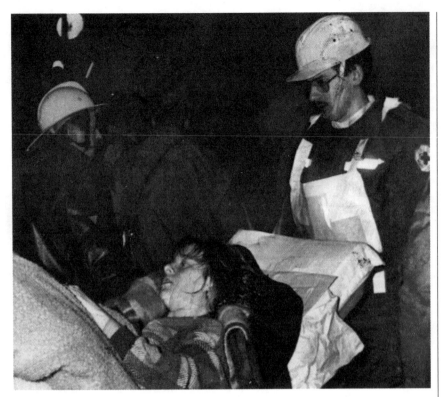

*Above: The ferry lurched like a giant whale, throwing passengers across decks, shops, lounges, bars and restaurants. The injured were carried out shocked and disorientated.*

looked back at it, it looked like something out of the Second World War that was hit with torpedoes.'

---

A lorry driver looked back and thought the stricken ship looked as if she had been hit by torpedoes

---

Many of the people on board were day trippers taking advantage of an offer from Britain's biggest popular newspaper, the *Sun,* to sail cheaply, on a day return ticket costing £1. One of them, Andrew Simmons, 30, of Bushey, near Watford, recalled: 'We were trapped for twenty or thirty minutes after the boat went over. Within a minute it went from being upright to on its side with water gushing in down the stairs and corridors. I and my friend helped a little girl, who was only two or three years old, climb up with her father above the water. We were only rescued when people smashed the windows from outside and hauled us out to safety.'

### THE HEROES

Many individual acts of heroism were performed that night, not least among them that of Londoner Andrew Parker. In the pitch dark, with a cold black sea rising, carrying with it the wreckage of furniture, old bottles, discarded lifejackets and fuel oil, this brave man turned himself into a human ladder bridging a gap over the water, thus allowing 120 people to clamber over him to safety. He would later be awarded the George Medal for bravery. To this day the nightmare of what happened haunts him and he suffers from post-traumatic stress disorder.

---

When one man offered himself as a human ladder, more than a hundred people scrambled over him to safety

---

bridge as the *Herald* pulled away from pier 12 at five minutes past six.

Four hundred and thirty-six passengers were on board that night, many of them on the deck watching the twinkling lights of Zeebrugge recede in the distance. In her belly were nearly forty trucks and over eighty cars. For a vessel that could comfortably accommodate a thousand people she was, with her eighty crewmen on top of the passenger complement, marginally over half full.

Barely twenty minutes later the crowded bar, restaurant, duty-free shop, lounges and decks were turned into a maelstrom of nightmare panic as the ship violently listed and then lurched like a giant whale on to her side. It was the start of a night of hell.

As the vessel listed over many passengers were simply sucked out of the windows through sheer force. Larry O'Brian, a lorry driver from Ireland, was sitting in the ship's restaurant when he suddenly saw plates and china fly from the tables. He said: 'In forty-five seconds the boat was on its side and half-filled with water. People were sucked out through portholes like you see in those movies about air disasters. They didn't have a chance. And the boat - well, when I was being taken off it and I

Another hero was Lieutenant Guido Couwenbergh a Belgian Navy frogman one of the first on the scene. Singlehandedly he saved forty people from drowning. He received the Queen's Gallantry Medal.

Couwenbergh and his colleagues

arrived in naval helicopters whose rotors whined noisily above the screams of the trapped and dying below. For them, it was a race against time.

As with the passengers who died in the stricken *Titanic* seventy-five years before them, the cold sea threatened to claim even the strongest swimmer with hypothermia in minutes. One teenager, Nicola Simpson, from Hertfordshire, was clinically dead with a body temperature 25 degrees below normal after she was rescued by Belgian civilian diver Piet Lagast. She was even certified dead on arrival at a Belgian hospital, but thanks to sterling efforts by doctors and nurses who worked throughout the night to raise her temperature, she survived.

Nicola and eight others were trapped behind a sheet of thick glass in the ship that Lagast shattered with his diver's knife - almost severing his hand in the process. He too was a recipient of the Queen's Gallantry Medal.

Massive sodium arc lights were brought to play on the corpse of the doomed vessel as wire reports clattered into TV and newspaper offices around the world. Anguished relatives at Dover docks who besieged the Townsend Thoresen offices attacked pressmen who descended there to cover the worst tragedy in British maritime history in years.

---

**The water was so cold that hospital staff laboured for hours to bring one young girl back from clinical death**

---

The Royal Navy was on hand to help in the shape of HMS *Glasgow* and HMS *Diomede,* assisting helicopters from naval squadrons based at Culdrose as they hovered over the living and the dead in the sea. A pilot was later to say: 'I could see black shapes bobbing in the water, arms splayed out like jellyfish and I knew they were the dead.'

THE DOORS THAT NO ONE CLOSED

Daylight brought the real tragedy of Zeebrugge home to the world. Stabilized by tugs, the hulk rested in shallow water on a sandbar with the sea

*Below: A floating crane comes alongside the* **Herald of Free Enterprise.** *Only when righted was the full horror inside revealed.*

**Left:** *The first articulated truck is lifted from the vehicle deck of the capsized ferry. Many of the dead and injured were lorry drivers.*

**Below:** *It looked like a wreckers' yard. But these were the cars and trucks of passengers trapped within the freezing, black, waterlogged hulk of the channel ferry.*

coming roughly halfway up her hull. At the front of the ship, plain for all to see and obviously the cause of the disaster, were the cargo deck doors wide open. It was apparent in those hours after the accident that there was an awful lot of explaining to do on someone's behalf.

The captain, David Lewry, as master of his ship, ultimately takes the blame. But the public inquiry which followed proved that the *Herald of Free Enterprise*'s demise rested on far more than one man's shoulders.

It exposed a management system that was out of touch with the day-to-day operations of its fleet and crewmen who were negligent in their duties.

In July 1987, after a twenty-nine-day inquiry, Mr Justice Sheen, who chaired the investigation, concluded that: 'From top to bottom the body was infected by the disease of sloppiness.' Four men, including Captain Lewry, were singled out for making the fatal mistakes which had led to the tragedy. The others were: Senior Master John Kirby, Assistant Boatswain Mark Stanley and Chief Officer Leslie Sabel. Mr Justice Sheen stated plainly what the cause of the accident was.

'The *Herald* sank because she went to sea with her inner and outer bow doors open.' But he went on to say: 'A full investigation into the circumstances of the disaster leads inexorably to the conclusion that the underlying or cardinal faults lay higher up the company.'

It was learned that Mark Stanley, in charge of closing the doors before the ship put to sea, had been asleep at the time. He only woke up as he was thrown from his bunk when the ship keeled over. Leslie Sabel was criticized because he did not check that the doors were shut before sailing. Various captains in the past had expressed concern about the practice of setting sail with the bow doors open to Townsend management in memos. At least one of them expressed the opinion that indicator lights were needed on the bridge to show whether or not bow doors had been closed. The inquiry said that this idea deserved 'serious consideration' - consideration that it had previously not received.

---

The indirect blame for the tragedy was laid firmly at the feet of sloppy management

---

He went on to say that Captain Lewry ultimately had to carry the burden of responsibility. 'Captain Lewry took the *Herald* to sea with the bow doors fully open. It follows that Captain Lewry must accept personal responsibility for the loss of his ship.' In mitigation it had to be borne in mind, said the judge, that the skipper was working to the same system that existed on other company ships, and that there were no standing orders to close the bow and stern doors.

And he was scathing in his criticism of Townsend's bosses for 'staggering complacency', which led to a 'malaise' which infected it.

After the inquiry, an inquest at Dover ruled that the passengers were the victims of unlawful killing. Charges were later brought against both crewmen and

management, but were later dropped. The memory of what had happened was to be punishment enough.

### THE LEGACY

The legacy of the *Herald* disaster was a change in ships' operating procedures. Under maritime law it would be an offence for a vessel to set sail again in a similar fashion.

For the survivors there are only bitter memories left: of loved ones, including Nicola Simpson's mother, who were lost; for crewmen, who saw twelve of their shipmates go down; for Captain Lewry, who in the immediate aftermath of the accident wished he were dead.

The battered and scarred hull of the ship was finally taken apart in a scrapyard in Taiwan.

**Above:** *Giant floating cranes had to be brought in to raise the* Herald of Free Enterprise. *Her battered hulk was later taken apart in a scrapyard in Taiwan.*

# ABERFAN SCHOOL
## Disaster in the Valleys

The people of coal-mining areas are used to tragedy. But the little village of Aberfan in South Wales was visited by one more terrible than anyone could have imagined when a slagheap engulfed the school and took its children

The story of Wales is written in tragedy. The dark valleys have been witness to much suffering: hardship on the land, poverty in the homes, danger and death in the mines. Above it all, its people have remained strong and proud, descendants of hardy tribes who cherished their Welsh heritage despite its often uncompromising face.

But there is not a man or woman alive who could have foreseen that the greatest tragedy ever to strike Wales would occur in the village of Aberfan - the victim of the mountain that moved to claim the lives of a generation of children. In every sense they were the victims of the

*Above: The close-knit community toiled day and night to recover bodies from their black tomb.*

*Opposite: At 7.30am on 21 October 1966 the mountain of sludge known as Tip No. 7 began to slide towards the village of Aberfan.*

*Below: One of the victims is carried to an ambulance from the buried school.*

pits as much as their fathers and grandfathers - smothered by the very spoil that they had gouged from the earth in order to earn a living.

Aberfan bears the scars of the tragedy to this day, and it is not a village that one can easily feel comfortable in.

The tragedy began at precisely 7.30am on 21 October 1966. Tip no. 7, in National Coal Board parlance, sat like a black cancer on the side of Merthyr Mountain, 500 ft up in the mists and light rain that began to fall as the town stirred for another day. It had rained for weeks, the water acting like a loosening agent on the foul-smelling muck which besmirched the side of the mountain.

At that moment the black slurry began to move, its enormous weight shifting with all the creaks and groans of the beginning of a giant slide. Some 100,000 tons of rocks and mud, hewn by miners from the pits below and around, suddenly began its inexorable journey to the unsuspecting community below.

Little Paul Davies was one of the scabby-kneed kids of Aberfan who was in the Pantglas infants' and junior school at the foot of the mountain - one of a cluster of buildings that included a row of cottages and a farm. Five-year-old Paul loved drawing, and was sketching even as the unstoppable slurry was gathering momentum, moving faster and faster for its appointment with catastrophe. He drew clockfaces, all of them saying 9.25. One picture showed a mountain of sludge

Survivors recall hearing the screech of dragged gravel and breaking rocks reaching a crescendo shortly before it broke over the village below.

### THE TERRIBLE DEATH TOLL

The Rev. Kenneth Hayes remembers those split seconds with awful clarity. It is a moment in time that will never leave him. He rounded the corner of a street to see a mound of slurry climbing up the outside of the school building before the sheer weight behind it pushed it through on its lethal mission. His nine-year-old son Dyfig was among those it claimed.

'The slurry just overwhelmed the school,' he said. 'I saw the last of the living being taken out and the first of the dead. I knew I had lost my boy, although his body was not found until the following day. That was when the enormity of it all dawned on us. Whole families had been wiped out. I buried five from one house that Thursday.'

Phillip Thomas remembers crying as the stones crushed his hands, and calling out desperately for his 'mam'. He had left the school on an errand with another boy, and so was out of the classroom when the wall of mud smashed into it. He recalled:

*I was buried immediately and found myself crying. Then all I remember was men digging me out, and muddy water was pouring, pouring all over me. Robert, the boy on the errand, was found two days later - dead. My right hand was crushed so badly I lost three fingers. My leg was injured, my pelvis fractured, my hair gone. I had bleeding internally and externally and they said I would have bled to death if the mud hadn't caked on me, forming a skin. The force of the mud was such that it smashed my spleen, which had to be removed, and ripped off an ear, which had to be sewn back on.*

---

One boy would have bled to death if the mud had not formed a protective cake over his injuries

---

Susan Maybank, nearly eight years old, was sitting in her classroom. Her teacher glanced out of the window just as he saw the merciless black monster

**Above:** *Rescue workers dig among the rubble after the rain-soaked coal tip avalanched onto the infants' school.*

sliding onto his school while a plane marked 'National Coal Board' dropped bombs on to the mountain.

At 9.25am the moving mountain hit Pantglas infants' school. Later, when they pulled little Paul's smothered body from underneath the school clock, it was stuck at 9.25.

The tide of sludge had hit with the force of a hurricane, smothering, smashing, crushing everything in its path.

**Right:** *Prince Philip, Duke of Edinburgh, rushed to the scene to talk to rescue workers and comfort relatives of the dead.*

about to engulf the school, and shouted a warning for her and her classmates to dive under their desks.

Seconds later, as the children - some of them believing they were playing an exciting new game - were on all fours, the slurry smashed through the walls as if they were paper. The teacher died instantly, and Susan remembers being engulfed by the cold blackness.

She has no idea how long she was underground - all she remembers was pushing her fingers through the muck to form an air-hole and waving them around. The small army of men - pensioners, off-duty miners, policemen, firemen, builders, doctors, solicitors, bakers and cooks - that had descended on the school to begin frantically clawing at the rubble with their bare hands rescued her. In the slime were her best friends, entombed forever.

Eye-witnesses to the tragedy will never forget the scene of the sweating, wet-eyed men, their limbs trembling with rage and fury, their hands bleeding.

Elizabeth Jones was trapped for several hours with the dead body of another child jammed up against her. Now aged thirty-one, she believes she

**Above:** *Bereaved families weep at the communal grave where eighty tiny coffins were laid to rest side by side.*

**Right:** *A shocked world reacted immediately to the disaster by sending thousands of consoling letters containing hard-earned cash and cheques for the Aberfan Disaster Fund.*

escaped because she left a classroom to take her dinner money along to the school office when it happened.

'I only remember being engulfed in masonry and sludge,' she said.

*I was trapped in the school corridor for a long time with the body of a little boy beneath me and by the side of me. When they pulled me out I was still holding my shilling dinner money. I am sure that saved me and I still keep it as a lucky coin.*

*Another souvenir is the plaster cast which my leg was in for months afterwards. Most of my memories have mercifully faded - when your mind luckily begins to think of other things. But I received severe internal injuries in the slide and as a result will never be able to have children.*

All day and into the night the frantic struggle for survivors went on. Lord Snowdon and the ashen-faced Secretary of State for Wales, George Thomas, arrived to see the pathetic bodies of the children being plucked one by one from the black sea.

Later the agony was too much even for hardened journalists to bear as the children's pathetic corpses were laid in the Morriah Chapel for their agonized parents to come and identify them. An anguished keening rose into the skies above Aberfan that day: 'Why us, oh Lord, why us?'

By nightfall the generators hummed as the sodium arc lamps threw their light on the shattered school and surrounding buildings. Still the remains of tip no. 7 continued to yield casualties up from its smothering clutches.

Bryn Carpenter was in hospital the morning of the slide, recovering from a pit accident himself. He was rushed to the scene and found a sight more terrifying than anything he had ever witnessed below ground. He said:

*We believed our ten-year-old Desmond was buried in there. When they told us of an unidentified ten-year-old in hospital our spirits lifted, but it turned out to be someone else.*

*Later that night they found Desmond's body. We were by no means alone in our grief. In my street alone we lost fourteen. Two houses lost two children each. And time doesn't heal - there is always something there to trigger grief again.*

One of the lucky ones was Pat Lewis, whose eldest sister Sharon was killed in the slime that she managed to escape from. Just a week shy of her ninth birthday, she saw the wall splitting behind the teacher as he stood up to call the names on the morning register. Her shouted warning enabled him to get many of the children outside, and she was saved.

Her mother, Sheila, scooped her in her arms as she arrived home - apologizing because her coat was still in the school. Sheila, a trained nurse, went back with her to the school and climbed in through a broken window. She recalled:

*Inside were about twenty children who had been swept forward by the fast-approaching tip as it bulldozed the building. They were the ones who could be helped, though one of those children walked out of the ruins, seemingly all right, then collapsed and died.*

*I laid the survivors on blankets in the school yard and turned the infants' classroom into a first aid post. I worked the whole day but nobody came out alive after 11am. It was the most horrifying day, but your senses sharpen at times like that and so I can remember it all clearly.*

*I knew I couldn't go and identify Sharon's body. My poor husband had to go and do it. He came back from the chapel at about 5am on Saturday and*

**Below: *Homes too were destroyed as the killer coal slagheap swept past the infants' school and engulfed part of the village.***

**Above:** *A touching tribute to the eighty children who perished. This giant Cross of Aberfan was made out of wreaths and flowers on a hillside overlooking the cemetery.*

**Left:** *Villagers openly wept as they witnessed bodies being brought out of the rubble and mud that was once a village school.*

*said he recognized her. She had been found with the rest of the class and the teacher. I was sitting on a stool by the fire and I remember I slid back against the wall and made a terrible noise for I don't know how long.*

Body after tiny body was laid in the chapel, their eyes and mouths filled with coal slurry that parents angrily cleaned out so their loved ones could rest with dignity. Throughout the night the parents came, and Aberfan was plunged into the post-shock trauma of a town that had suffered and lost on a tremendous scale. The final tally of dead was 144. Of the 116 schoolchildren, most of them were under the age of ten.

Afterwards, of course, bureaucrats moved in for the biggest government inquiry ever held. It lasted five months, and heard evidence from 136 witnesses.

Controversially the Coal Board chairman Alfred Robens, later Lord Robens, stayed away - although he attended later as the community felt painfully snubbed by his absence.

Due to goodness knows what rules of accounting, the government paid out £500 to each family that had lost a child. A further £5000 went to each family from a special fund patronized by the Queen, Prince Philip and Prince Charles.

## THE TRAGEDY THAT SHOULD NEVER HAVE HAPPENED

There was only one verdict - that it could have all been prevented.

It emerged that there was no national safety policy for tips like Aberfan. The Coal Board was held to be legally liable for what had happened when it emerged that mandarins in the industry had ignored warnings about the dangerous state of the Aberfan tip since as far back as 1960.

---

Warnings about the state of the tip at Aberfan had been ignored for the previous six years.

---

Lord Robens had to live with the memory of what had happened to Aberfan, with the knowledge that it need never have occurred. In 1986, when newspapers around the world ran a retrospective on the tragedy to mark its twentieth anniversary, he said:

*The one question I constantly turn over in my mind is how it could have been prevented. There were thousands of pit heaps all over the country and they all came within the local pit authority's guidelines. It is awful that it takes something like that to make sure every safety regulation is double-checked and brought into practice.*

*When I think of all I did during my time with the Coal Board it diminishes to nothing when I think of the Aberfan disaster. It is a terrible thing which will always haunt me.*

On the bleak hillside above Aberfan stands one of the most poignant sights in Britain - row upon row of children's gravestones, the victims of the moving mountain that claimed them that day.

# MI5 SPY RING
# A Web of Deception

# The sensational defection of Burgess and Maclean in 1951 triggered the exposure of a web of espionage and double dealing. For decades Englishmen in high places had been spying for the Russians

It was in the unlikely surroundings of Cambridge University that the twentieth century's most dangerous spy ring was spawned. In the 1930s as ex-public schoolboys punted down the River Cam, they formed the idea that Communism provided a better life and a stronger way to fight Fascism.

A former Russian envoy to London had started the recruitment ball rolling. Maxim Litvinov theorized that these undergraduates, already on the lower rungs of the Establishment ladder, would never have their loyalty doubted. So the Russian net was cast.

And within just a few years it hauled in a group of Cambridge students. Guy Burgess, Donald Maclean, Anthony Blunt and Kim Philby were to cause untold damage to Britain. Many died because of their treachery. Yet none of the spies was ever brought to justice.

---

**In the thirties many undergraduates turned to Communism as a way of rejecting Fascism**

---

It was Blunt who led the way to Cambridge and to Trinity College, which was to have the dubious distinction of being the breeding ground for each of the traitors. The son of a vicar, brilliant and a homosexual, he arrived at Trinity in 1928. He was a gifted student in mathematics, languages and art, and after he graduated he became a teaching Fellow.

**Above:** *Anthony Blunt's shame as a Soviet spy went unrevealed for years. He continued in his post as adviser to the Queen on her fabulous art collection.*

**Opposite:** *Kim Philby holds a press conference after he was wrongly cleared of being the 'Third Man' in the Burgess-Maclean affair.*

**Right:** *Foreign office intelligence chief Donald Maclean in a conference with the then British Ambassador to Washington, Sir John Balfour.*

Harold Philby - nicknamed Kim - arrived in 1929. And a year later they were joined by old Etonian Guy Francis de Moncy Burgess, an eccentric homosexual with a large capacity for alcohol and indiscreet gossip. Donald Maclean, the son of a religious Liberal cabinet minister, arrived in 1931.

Many Trinity College students became Communists. But for most it was a passing phase. For these four it became their life's work.

After university Maclean went to the Foreign Office. One of his interviewers,

he later said, asked him: 'We understand that you held strong Communist views while you were at Cambridge. Do you still hold those views?'

'I decided to brazen it out. "Yes," I said "I did have such views - and I haven't entirely shaken them off." They must have liked my honesty.'

After Trinity, Burgess talked his way into a job with Tory MP Jack Macnamara. Burgess had already visited Russia and had met spy chiefs to arrange his contacts in London. He and Blunt became the organizers of the spy ring.

He was making contacts all the time and as war approached he became a secret courier carrying messages to European leaders. All the information he gained he was passing back to his Soviet spymasters. But at the same time he was feeding tip-offs to British Intelligence. His devious hard work paid off. In January 1939 MI6 offered him a staff job.

After Cambridge Philby went to Vienna, where he helped Communists to escape from the Nazis. He reappeared in London with a wife – a Soviet spy – and began to cultivate a right-wing image. In 1937 he went to Spain to cover the Civil War for the *Times* as a reporter. It was a useful cover to feed back information to the Russians, who were supporting the Republicans.

### WAR WORK

In 1939 Blunt applied for a five-week military intelligence course. His Marxist past caught up with him, and he was returned to his unit as a 'security risk'.

But he wasn't downhearted by his first failure to infiltrate the security services. He joined the Army's Intelligence Corps and was evacuated from Dunkirk. And then, via the 'old boy' network, he was recruited by MI5.

Philby's chance to infiltrate the Secret Services came with a surprise phone call in June 1940 from the War Office. He was offered a job in Section D, in a new department formed to cause subversive chaos in Europe. His interviewers for the job included one Guy Burgess! And he soon progressed into MI6.

The job of MI5 was to protect security at home, while MI6 was in charge of

**Right:** *Donald Maclean in characteristic pose. This was the elegant Englishman who traded life in the West for a mundane existence behind the Iron Curtain.*

**Opposite:** *'Fourth Man' Anthony Blunt with the three defectors from British intelligence in the fifties and sixties - Guy Burgess, Donald Maclean and Kim Philby.*

**Below:** *A gardener tends the grounds of Maclean's house in Tatsfield, Kent, while the hunt goes on for the missing diplomat.*

intelligence-gathering abroad. Already Guy Burgess was hard at work for his Russian bosses.

Soviet Embassy cipher clerks were working full-time to encode the mass of material for transmission to Moscow.

Philby started by sending lists of agents, codenames and wavelengths from the central archives of the Secret Intelligence Services.

And from inside MI5 Blunt made sure that Russian atom spies Dr Klaus Fuchs and Dr Alan Nunn May could continue their work on the atom bomb – despite their obvious Communist leanings.

**Above:** *Maclean sent telegrams from Paris in 1951. To his mother he said: 'Am quite all right.' To his wife he said: 'Don't stop loving me.'*

**Left:** *Guy Burgess's mother, Mrs Jack Bassett in 1956.*

**Below:** *Guy Burgess (left)* with **Daily Express** *man Terence Lancaster in Moscow in 1957.*

At the same time as supporting these two scientists Blunt was accepting a new job - as Surveyor of the King's Pictures. His disloyalty knew no bounds.

In 1944 Maclean was appointed Head of Chancery at the British Embassy in Washington. One of his first calls was to the Soviet Consulate to meet his new controller.

He would have a lot of information to give him. Memos between Roosevelt and Churchill outlining war plans and post-war policy crossed his desk. And then after World War II Maclean was made secretary of the committee that dealt as the clearing house for atomic bomb information between the Western allies.

Meanwhile Philby had been promoted to a plum job too. He was made head of Section Nine, the department controlling espionage against Russia. It meant that Russia was warned of every planned spying mission against them.

### RUMOURS AND DANGERS

The sheer bulk of information that the four were providing meant that suspicions were bound to be aroused. It was the Americans who first asked: why do the Russians know everything we're doing, before we've done it?

There was one specific case that threatened to uncover Philby. In August 1945 the Secret Service received a message that KGB man Konstantin Volkov wanted to defect to Britain with his wife. In return he promised to reveal the name of three British spies working for the Soviets in the Foreign Office and the Secret Service. Luckily for Philby, he was given the case to handle personally.

---

When a Russian defector offered to unmask British moles, it was Philby who was put in charge of the case!

---

When Philby arrived in Turkey, where he was supposed to meet the Russian, Volkov did not appear. He was next seen in Moscow – with a bullet in the back of his head. Years later the cynical Philby explained: 'It was either Volkov's head or mine.' And despite US suspicions, he got away with it.

After the war Burgess entered the

Foreign Office and became personal assistant to Hector MacNeil, the Labour government's deputy Foreign Secretary.

But the strain was telling on Burgess and Maclean and they were turning to drink. Maclean was sent to Cairo. But it didn't stop his boozing. After a drunken rampage, during which he snatched a nightwatchman's gun and then broke his leg, he was sent back to Britain.

By 1950 Burgess was in a terrible state. An official report on him stated: 'The sooner we get rid of this appalling man the better for all of us.' Wherever he went, he engaged in drinking bouts and fights. He launched vicious attacks on British policy. Still in August 1950 he was posted to Washington as first secretary. There he joined Philby, who had been appointed MI6's liaison man with the CIA.

But the noose around the spy ring's neck was tightening. Philby had already warned Burgess that British security was closing in on Foreign Office suspects.

In Washington he took Burgess under his wing - and under his roof. It was his last chance, the Foreign Office had decided. But both Burgess and Philby were still passing useful information to the Russians in Washington.

### ESCAPE TO THE EAST

By 1951 Philby knew, because of his privileged position, that Maclean was close to being exposed. What he did not know was that the Americans had also targeted him and Burgess.

Maclean had to be warned, and had to escape. If he was captured he was bound to talk - he had become a nervous wreck. Philby nominated Burgess as messenger, but he could not return to Britain without an official reason. He contrived a series of embarrassing incidents, so the Ambassador had to order him home.

It was Blunt who discovered from his MI5 contacts the exact time when 'Homer' - the mole's codename - was to be picked up. On 25 May 1951 Foreign Secretary Herbert Morrison signed the paper ordering Maclean's interrogation.

Burgess knew within minutes and contacted Maclean. On the pretext of taking a holiday, they boarded a ferry to

**Above:** *Donald Maclean's wife Melinda arrives back from France with her family after the disappearance of her husband.*

**Left:** *The Maclean family car was found eight days after his disappearance, in a Lausanne garage.*

France that night. Neither was to be seen in Britain again. Their next public appearance was in 1956, when they were paraded in Moscow as heroes of the Communist struggle.

Why Burgess joined Maclean in his flight has never been revealed. He probably panicked. Their hurried flight left the remaining two Cambridge spies to face the music.

### THE CHARMED LIFE OF A TRAITOR

It took a matter of hours for the authorities to link Philby with Burgess and Maclean's sudden disappearance. He was summoned back to London by MI6 chief Sir Stewart Menzies. Somehow Philby brazened it out, putting the blame

At Cambridge we had both been communists. We abandoned our political activities not because we disagreed with the Marxist analysis of the world situation, in which we still all find ourselves, but because we thought, wrongly it is now clear to us, that in the public service we could do more to put these ideas into practical effect than elsewhere.

It is probably our action in necessarily giving up political activities by entering the public service that, falsely analysed the Foreign Office to say through its spokesman that it "believed" we had been Soviet agents at Cambridge. The Foreign Office can of course "believe" anything it wishes. The important point however is that on this question we know, and it does not. We neither of us have ever been communist agents.

So far the ground was common for us both. The details of our subsequent careers were completely different and had therefore better be dealt with separately.

As regards Maclean, he worked in London and in Paris, Washington and Cairo as a regular member of the Foreign Service

**Above:** *The signed thousand-word statement of Burgess and Maclean. In it they say: 'Neither of us have ever been Communist agents.'*

**Right:** *Mrs Philby and a journalist in Beirut. She had reported her husband's disappearance but then heard that he had fled to Moscow.*

fairly and squarely on the now absent Burgess. Philby was allowed to resign and take a £4000 golden handshake.

In his wake he left chaos. Ten intelligence service officials were forced to resign - not for being moles, but for failing to prevent spying.

In 1955 the government published the long-awaited White Paper on the disappearance of Burgess and Maclean. It was a whitewash. One MP described it as 'an insult to the intelligence of the country'.

But the most dangerous moment came for Philby when MP Marcus Lipton tabled a parliamentary question. The MP, primed by MI5, asked Tory Prime Minister Sir Anthony Eden: 'Have you made up your mind to cover up at all costs the dubious third man activities of Harold Philby?'

---

In 1955 Philby was named as the Third Man. Despite government warnings, MI6 continued to use him as an agent

---

For the first time Philby had been named as the so-called Third Man. And because the question was covered by parliamentary privilege the press could report it without running the risk of libel.

Foreign Secretary Harold Macmillan answered the question and told the House the conclusions of the Foreign Service's investigations:

*I have no reason to conclude that Mr Philby has at any time betrayed the interests of this country, or to identify him with the so-called 'Third Man', if indeed there was one....*

Philby was cock-a-hoop and held a press conference to celebrate. 'I have never been a Communist,' he lied.

MI6 took all this as a cue to use Philby as an agent again, when he was in the Middle East as a reporter for the *Observer* newspaper. There he began to feed the Soviets information again.

### THE NET CLOSES

But Philby could not escape the truth for ever. MI5 still insisted that Philby was a mole, and final proof came with the sudden defection of Russian KGB man Anatoli Golitsin. He identified Philby as the Third Man beyond doubt.

In January 1963 agent Nicholas Elliott, an old friend of Philby's, flew to confront him with the new evidence.

'You took me in for years,' he said. 'Now I'll get the truth out of you even if I have to drag it out. I once looked up to you, Kim. God, how I despise you now.'

The Attorney-General, Sir John Hobson, had agreed that the spy could be offered immunity from prosecution - in exchange for a full confession.

He revealed how he had been recruited and trained, and detailed his work as a double agent. But he refused to name his contacts and to sign a written confession.

As Elliott returned to England for further instructions, Philby fled. In July the Supreme Soviet granted Philby's request for political asylum. Not only that, they gave him Russian citizenship and a job in the KGB as well!

## THE MOLE AT THE PALACE

His escape left only the aesthetic intellectual Anthony Blunt still in place. Blunt had worked closely with Burgess, and now he feared that he would blurt out the truth from the safety of Moscow - to where Blunt had refused to flee.

By the time that Blunt faced William Skardon, the ace interrogator, he had already been questioned eleven times. This time though, he was faced with harder evidence. After being offered immunity, and after pouring himself a stiff drink, he then poured out his entire confession.

But astonishingly, despite his confession, the spy was allowed to keep his job as Surveyor of the Queen's Pictures and often met her in the course of his duties.

It was not until fourteen years later that Premier Margaret Thatcher was forced to act when the truth was uncovered by author Andrew Boyle. She announced: 'In April 1964, Sir Anthony Blunt admitted to the security authorities that he had passed information regularly to the Russians when he was a member of the Security Services...'

Minutes later Buckingham Palace announced that Blunt had been stripped of his knighthood.

---

**The Queen was informed that her art advisor was a self-confessed spy**

---

The so-called Mole at the Palace was finally exposed. He died disgraced seven years later, unloved save by his long-term homosexual partner, John Gaskin. At his funeral Blunt's brother Christopher said 'Anthony bitterly regretted that he got it wrong. But he was not ashamed. He was on the tiger and could not get off.' Burgess had died earlier, in 1963, homesick and an alcoholic. Maclean died in the same month as Blunt. Philby continued working for the KGB until the very end.

He swore that the only things he missed about Britain were the cricket scores and marmalade. But in 1982 a Russian freighter was spotted moored off the Sussex coast. On the bridge with a pair of binoculars was a stooped figure. It was Philby, taking a last longing look.

He died in Moscow in May 1988 and was given a full military send-off in Moscow's Kuntsevo cemetery.

**Above:** *Kim Philby with his mother in November 1955.*

**Below:** *Anthony Blunt addresses a press conference in London in 1980. He tried to fudge the accusations that he was the long-sought 'Fourth Man' in Britain's worst espionage ring.*

# TENERIFE
# Take-off to Tragedy

On a foggy day in 1977 two jumbos were diverted to a small, single-runway airport in the Canaries. As a result nearly six hundred people died in the worst airline disaster the world has ever known

Pan American pilot Victor Grubbs carefully taxied his fully loaded 747 along the runway at Los Rodeos airport, waiting for the all-clear for take-off. But as he steered the giant craft down the runway, he could scarcely believe what he saw through the cockpit window. Some 350 yards away he saw the lights of another 747, owned by the Dutch airline KLM, emerge from the fog.

At first, both Captain Grubbs and his flight crew thought the other plane was parked, but as the lights drew brighter it became terrifyingly clear that the Dutch jumbo was heading straight for them at 160 mph.

'We are still on the runway!' Grubbs screamed to the air traffic controllers in the tower. 'What's he doing? He'll kill us all!' His co-pilot, Robert Bragg, yelled for him to 'Get off! Get off!'

Desperately, Captain Grubbs swerved sharply to the left, heading for the grassy shoulder just off the runway. Tragically, he was a few seconds too late, as the KLM liner crashed broadside into the Pan Am clipper. Within seconds, the airstrip became a mass of tangled metal,

**Above:** *The arid peaks whose height causes the thick fogs that so often blank out Tenerife's airspace.*

**Opposite:** *The tailplane of the Pan Am jumbo jet after the worst air disaster in history.*

**Below:** *Tenerife is a sunny haunt for holidaymakers and the business heart of the Canary Islands.*

exploding fuel tanks and burning flesh.

It was 27 March 1977 - a day that saw the death of 583 Dutch and American citizens in the worst aviation disaster that had ever taken place.

### BITTER IRONY

The tragedy was filled with the most bitter of ironies: neither plane had even intended stopping at Los Rodeos, a second-rate airport that was never considered among the safest in the region. But a terrorist bomb had exploded at their original destination, the more modern facility at Las Palmas some 70 miles away, and for safety's sake both aircraft had been rerouted to Tenerife.

That day had begun in a mood of innocent good humour. The Dutch airliner was carrying 283 holidaymakers, eager to begin their Easter break on Las Palmas.

The Pan Am clipper was carrying 380 passengers to a rendezvous with the cruise ship *Golden Odyssey*.

---

**The disaster would never have happened if Las Palmas airport had not been closed due to a terrorist bomb**

---

The re-routing seemed no more than a minor inconvenience, and both jumbos landed without incident. Captain Grubbs taxied his clipper, Victor, up to the terminal building and parked it alongside another 747, the Rhine, skippered by Captain Jacob Louis Veldhuyzen van Zanten, KLM's chief jumbo instructor.

Once the Rhine had been refuelled, Captain Veldhuyzen van Zanten asked for flight clearance. According to aviation officials, at Los Rodeos a plane would normally taxi its way to the southeast corner of the field for take-off, but because of the emergency at Las Palmas that route was now crowded by other diverted planes. So the tower instructed the KLM plane to taxi up the runway itself, and at the end Veldhuyzen van Zanten made a 180-degree turn and prepared for take-off.

At the same time, the tower instructed Grubbs too to taxi up the runway, but told him to turn off by the third exit on his left, thus leaving the airstrip free for the

KLM jumbo. A few minutes later, controllers asked him if he had made the turn. When Grubbs replied that he hadn't, they told him: 'Do it, and advise when the runway is clear.'

But as the clipper continued up the runway, shrouded in mist and therefore invisible both to the Dutch plane and to the tower, the KLM crew made its last transmission to the tower: 'KLM....We are now ready on [or 'at' - the exact wording was garbled] take-off.'

Grubbs's worst nightmare was happening. The KLM was hurtling out of the fog at 160 mph, and heading straight for him. Frantically he radioed the tower

that he was still on the runway, then swore angrily as he desperately gunned his engines and jerked his plane to the left. As he did so, Veldhuyzen van Zanten urgently tried to take his plane into the air. Its nose lifted but the tail remained on the runway, digging an ugly, gaping trench.

## IMPACT

It smashed into the Pan Am jumbo in the forward part of the second-class section, while its right wing slashed through the bubble atop the cockpit, slicing off the roof. The Pan Am clipper, cut in half and already on fire, toppled to the side of the runway.

A split second later, the Dutch plane slammed back to the ground, skidded around backwards and screeched to a halt about 300 yards away. In an instant, it exploded into a ball of flames, the inferno gorging itself on its just-filled fuel tanks. Everyone on board was killed. The impact was so hard and the explosive fire so hot that aluminium and steel parts on both planes were vaporized.

Back on board the American plane, there was pandemonium. Debris seemed to be falling from everywhere, and the flames were quickly spreading. Terrified and dazed, those who could scrambled to get out. Many were already dead, and

*Above: The passengers who packed the Dutch and American jumbos had dreamed of lazing on sun-drenched beaches fanned by Atlantic breezes.*

others were too stunned to move.

Inside the twisted wreck, heroic thirty-three-year-old businessman Edgar Ridout tried to organize an evacuation.

---

Some of the Pan Am passengers were in such shock that they just stood there as if nothing had happened

---

The brave businessman helped one of the stewardesses inflate a life raft so that passengers could jump onto it as they leaped from the plane.

### HEROES AND SURVIVORS

There were many heroes that day. As burning debris and red-hot metal continued to shower the immediate area, melting the runway, Jack Daniel helped his wife and daughter to safety, then disappeared. His frightened wife began frantically asking if anyone had seen a man in a white suit. Someone answered that he had heard a woman screaming for help, and that a man in a white suit had raced back to help. Then there was another explosion, and both had disappeared.

Meanwhile, as the tragedy continued to unfold, doctors and nurses at the nearby La Candelaria Hospital began dealing with the wounded. Most of them had rushed to the hospital as word spread of the crash, and they worked gallantly under the most difficult conditions.

There were not enough beds for all the dying and the injured, so orderlies laid them on the floor while nurses scampered about handing out painkillers and sedatives and doctors began the task of stripping away burned skin.

Other survivors who had less serious injuries were huddled in the airport terminal. Blankets and painkillers were handed out to the stunned passengers, some of whom had had the clothes burned off their backs. Each of them spoke of their escape as miraculous. 'I felt someone was watching over me,' said Theresa Brusco. 'It was like we had a guardian angel around us.'

### WHAT WENT WRONG?

By this stage, scores of soldiers and police were combing through the gutted wreckage of both planes, engaged in the grisly task of sorting out bodies.

What had gone wrong? A horde of aviation experts from the United States, Holland and Spain quickly descended on Los Rodeos to find out, and at first suspicion fell on the air traffic controllers. It had been rumoured that they did not speak very good English - the language of international air traffic control - and that the two pilots might have been confused.

But that was quickly dispelled when investigators interviewed the three men who had been in the tower at the time of the crash. They all spoke 'textbook' English, and had followed take-off procedures to the letter.

The probe then targeted the captains, Grubbs and Veldhuyzen van Zanten.

At first, Dutch experts challenged the American flyer's conduct over the question of runway exits. There were four such exits along the runway, marked C-1 to C-4. KLM officials argued that Grubbs had been ordered to turn off at C-3 and that, had he done so, the catastrophe would never have occurred.

But Pan Am countered by claiming that their pilot had merely been told to

## THE VERDICT

It took an exhaustive, eighteen-month investigation before the Spanish government would release its findings.

The tragic verdict of the investigation was that Captain Veldhuyzen van Zanten had decided to start his take-off run without clearance, and that had been 'the fundamental cause'.

The report recalled that the weather was dismal that day, with low-scudding clouds and fog that sharply reduced visibility. But that on its own couldn't account for the Dutchman's strange and inexplicable decision.

How could a veteran pilot like Veldhuyzen van Zanten have made such an incredible mistake? It seems that, harried by an already lengthy delay on Tenerife and the erratic weather conditions, he may have rushed his take-off to avoid violating a KLM rule against crew overtime.

The radio 'whistle' could have beeped out some essential communications. And imprecise language used by both the tower and the KLM crew may have confused matters still further.

In the end, to those who died, it didn't matter...because just seconds later, the world's worst-ever aviation disaster occurred.

take 'the third exit' on the left. Pan Am executive William Waltrip asserted that C-1 was 'inactive', and that C-3 would have required an extremely difficult turn of 150 degrees. Therefore, the Americans maintained, the logical 'third exit' was C-4 - the one Grubbs never reached.

Moreover, argued the Americans, no matter where the clipper was supposed to be, Veldhuyzen van Zanten should never have taken off without clearance from the tower. The head of the Dutch investigation team had shocked his countrymen when he stated that he had found no clearance for the KLM take-off on the tower's nine-minute audio tape.

**Top:** *A memorial service for the victims of the disaster was conducted at Schiphol Airport, Amsterdam. On the runway were 232 coffins decked with flowers.*

**Above:** *Mourners leave the memorial service at Schiphol Airport.*

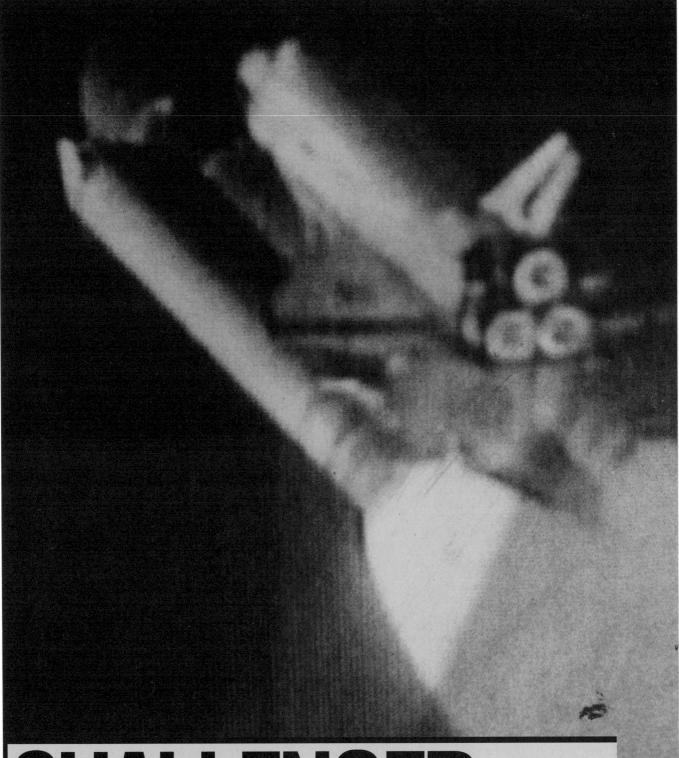

# CHALLENGER
# A Shattered Dream

In January 1986 a fireball of horror erupted into the sunny Florida skies. After twenty-five successful missions the Challenger space shuttle had blown up, killing all aboard her. What went wrong? And why were the warnings ignored?

The morning of 28 January 1986 began like many others for the skilled team of NASA scientists and engineers at Cape Canaveral, as they checked and rechecked the Space Shuttle *Challenger* in preparation for what they thought would be another routine mission in space for the reusable craft.

The seven astronauts - including Christa McAuliffe, who was to be the first civilian in space - were given last-minute briefings and instructions. And around the massive base, thousands of excited spectators and media representatives had gathered to await the spectacular launch.

None could have known that within seconds of that spectacular lift-off, the unthinkable would happen. The *Challenger* would explode in a fiery orange-and-white ball, killing all the crew members aboard and derailing the American space programme for almost three years.

In one tragic instant, the world's complacency towards manned space flight would evaporate forever nine miles up in the blue skies over Florida.

One spectator's scream was heard and repeated around the world: 'Oh, my God! What's happened?'

**Opposite:** *A moment of hope as* **Challenger** *takes to the skies. Within seconds came disaster.*

**Below:** *The* **Challenger's** *astronauts line up for the photo album before take-off from Cape Canaveral on 28 January 1986.*

### PRELUDE TO TRAGEDY

The story of *Challenger*'s fateful trip to oblivion began the previous night, as temperatures in the normally temperate Florida winter plunged to an unseasonable 27 degrees.

---

A spectator screamed: 'Oh, my God! What's happened?' Her agonized cry was heard by millions on TV worldwide

---

Early the next morning, NASA's so-called 'ice team' went to work, inspecting the shuttle for any signs of potentially dangerous build-ups of ice which could break away on lift-off and harm the *Challenger*'s heat-shield tiles.

It would later emerge that an engineer working with the Rockwell company in California, who had been watching the inspection on closed circuit television, called mission control to urge a delay because of the ice.

The gathered masses who stood cheering the astronauts as they walked to the *Challenger*, veteran of nine previous flights, knew nothing of the frantic warning which had come from three thousand miles away. Nor did the crew.

Once on board, they began their detailed checks of all systems with the aid of the craft's main computer.

Everything seemed right for the mission which included the deployment of a $100 million communications satellite into space and several on-board experiments. The astronauts were to measure the spectrum of Halley's comet; to sample radiation within the spacecraft at various points; and to examine the effects of weightlessness on the development of twelve chicken embryos.

---

From three thousand miles away came the unheeded advice to delay the launch because of the cold weather

---

At T minus seven minutes and thirty seconds the walkway was finally pulled away from the billion-dollar shuttle and its three huge engines.

The external tank stood more than ten storeys high and carried more than half a

**Above:** *The space shuttle lifts off from launch pad 39B. The orbiter craft carried the doomed crew of seven.*

million gallons of liquid oxygen and liquid hydrogen. The two booster rockets were packed with more than one million pounds of solid fuel.

The public address system continued: 'T minus forty-five seconds and counting,' as those in the huge crowd talked excitedly among themselves.

On board, Commander Dick Scobee and Pilot Michael Smith were strapped into the flight deck. Directly behind them were Judith Resnik, an electrical engineer, and Ronald McNair, a physicist. On the mid-deck below were Ellison Onizuka, an aerospace engineer,

Gregory Jarvis, an electrical engineer, and Christa McAuliffe.

With six seconds to go, the main engine was started. The roar was deafening.

'Four...three...two...one...and lift-off. Lift-off of the twenty-fifth space shuttle mission. And it has cleared the tower.' The spectators began to cheer wildly for the spectacular rise to the heavens.

Among those who watched the *Challenger*'s graceful ascent, its white plume of smoke shining brilliantly behind, were McAuliffe's family and eighteen of her third-grade class who had travelled some fifteen hundred miles from Concord, New Hampshire to see their teacher make history.

Sixteen seconds after launch the huge craft turned gracefully on its back as the main fuel tank and the two booster rockets assumed the course for leaving the earth's atmosphere. Mission control pronounced that all three engines were running smoothly.

'*Challenger*, go with throttle up,' said mission control exactly fifty-two seconds after launch. 'Roger, go with throttle up,' Scobee radioed back.

Three seconds later, NASA's long-range television cameras picked up an appallingly unfamiliar sight.

Television viewers could see what those below could not. A tiny but distinct orange glow flashed near the middle of the shuttle, between its underside and the external tank.

A split second later, the unthinkable nightmare happened. The *Challenger* was momentarily engulfed in flames, then disintegrated.

---

Unaware of the explosion, the official announcer continued his narration while the incredulous spectators watched in horror

---

Spectators felt an unspeakable horror as the hideous Y-shaped cloud spewed above them.

Incredibly, back at mission control in Houston, the official announcer had not been watching the TV monitor. Instead, he had his eyes glued on the programmed flight data displayed in front of him, and

reported what should have been the readings from *Challenger*.

'One minute, fifteen seconds. Velocity 2900 feet per second. Altitude nine nautical miles. Downrange distance seven nautical miles.' To the stunned millions watching on television, the narration was surreal.

Suddenly, he stopped. A minute later he announced: 'We have a report from the flight dynamics officer that the vehicle has exploded. The flight director confirms that.'

In Washington, President Ronald Reagan was working in the Oval Office when suddenly his top aides burst in.

'There's been a serious incident with the space shuttle,' said Vice President George Bush. Patrick Buchanan, the White House Communications Director, was much more blunt: 'Sir, the shuttle has exploded.'

Reagan, like the rest of America, was stunned. It was his decision that the first private citizen in space should be a schoolteacher. McAuliffe had been selected from more than eleven thousand hopeful applicants.

**Below:** *The view from Kennedy Space Center as* **Challenger** *explodes within moments of its launch.*

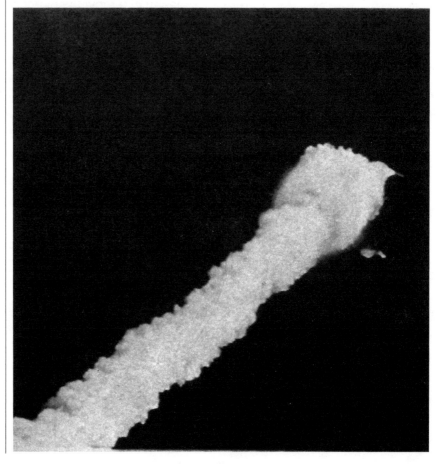

A few hours later he would try to soothe a grieving nation with a poignant speech in which he said that the seven pioneers had 'left the surly bonds of earth to touch the face of God'.

Then, addressing the nation's schoolchildren Reagan added: 'I know it's hard to understand that sometimes painful things like this happen. It's all part of the process of exploration...and expanding man's horizons.'

## GRIEF AND SORROW

Americans were shaken. Their scientists and astronauts had soared into space fifty-five times over the past quarter of a century, and their safe return had come to be taken for granted. An age when almost anyone, given a few months' training, could go along for a safe ride seemed at hand. McAuliffe, a vivacious high school teacher, was to be the standard bearer of that new era. Tragically, the era lasted just seventy-three seconds.

---

'They have left the surly bonds of earth to touch the face of God,' said President Reagan in a moving speech

---

After undergoing rigorous training for three months, the teacher was ready for her fantastic voyage. Her task was to conduct two fifteen-minute classes in space as millions of schoolchildren watched via closed circuit television. She would explain the functioning of the shuttle and the benefits of space travel.

She never got the chance to do what she loved best, which was to teach. Nowhere was the tragedy felt more than in Concord, where fellow teachers and pupils had gathered inside the school auditorium to watch what they had presumed to be their colleague and friend's moment of triumph.

Throughout the town, the thirty thousand residents were engulfed by sorrow as the news quickly spread. 'People froze in their tracks,' said one local. 'It was like part of the family has been killed.'

American music was played on Soviet state-run radio, and officials in Moscw announced they were naming craters on Venus in honour of the two female crew members, McAuliffe and Resnik.

In Vatican City, Pope John Paul II asked an audience of thousands to pray for the American astronauts, saying that the tragedy had 'provoked deep sorrow in my soul'. British Premier Margaret Thatcher sadly observed that 'New knowledge sometimes demands sacrifices of the bravest and the best.'

And Senator John Glenn, the first American to orbit the earth, recalled: 'The first group of us always knew there would be a day like this. We're dealing with speeds and powers and complexities we've never dealt with before.'

Across the United States, communities reacted in their own ways to the news. In Los Angeles, the Olympic torch atop the Coliseum was relit. New York City's Empire State Building was darkened. And along the Florida coast an estimated twenty-two thousand people pointed torches at the sky.

## THE INVESTIGATION

As the nation grieved, back at Cape Canaveral the US Coast Guard and NASA crews had already began the grim task of searching for the wreckage of *Challenger*.

They had to wait almost sixty minutes after the explosion before starting the search, because of debris still raining from the sky. Their search covered some six thousand square miles of the Atlantic.

Despite the power of the blast, searchers began finding surprisingly large parts of the wreckage scattered on the ocean floor, including a 25 ft long section of the *Challenger*'s fuselage.

As for the astronauts themselves, it was only after extensive prodding that NASA admitted that the crew had not perished instantly, as initially claimed. They survived the explosion and probably lived until their cabin hit the surface of the ocean.

Once the wreckage had been gathered, NASA investigators began the arduous task of finding out what had gone wrong. It was a three-pronged probe. First, there was the film to study from eighty NASA cameras and ninety belonging to news organizations. There were also the billions of computer signals sent between the doomed craft and its earthbound control centres. And lastly, there were the actual remains of the *Challenger*.

There was speculation that ice, which had formed on the launch pad the night before the lift-off, had damaged the craft - as the engineer at Rockwell had feared.

Also suspected was that the external fuel tank's insulation had been damaged during a minor accident a few days earlier, when a derrick arm supposedly scraped the tank. But NASA insisted the derrick had touched not the tank, but only part of the launch-pad equipment.

Speculation soon centred on the possibility of a failure in either the main tank or one of the two booster rockets. Experts noted that either could have caused the violent explosion. Another possibility was that a seam in the main tank had ruptured.

In closed meetings, a specially constituted panel began to grill top NASA officials as well as engineers from Morton Thiokol, the company that makes the solid fuel boosters suspected of triggering the disaster. What they uncovered stunned the commissioners.

The engineers had adamantly opposed the launch because of the icy weather at Cape Canaveral.

Robert Sieck, the shuttle manager at the Kennedy Space Center, and Gene Thomas, the launch director for *Challenger* at Kennedy, testified that they had never before heard that Thiokol engineers had objected to the launch.

Gradually, most rocket experts agreed that at least one of the two synthetic rubber O-rings that were meant to seal the joint between the booster's four segments had begun to burn. About 1/4 in thick, and some 37 feet in circumference, the O-rings are designed to keep the rocket's exhaust gases from escaping through any gaps in the joints.

The evening before the launch, Thiokol engineers and NASA officials met to discuss the potential problems. The engineers were unanimous in asking for the *Challenger* launch to be delayed.

They were worried that the O-rings might lose some of their elasticity, and hence their ability to sit tightly in their grooves around the rockets, when their temperature fell below 50 degrees. That evening the temperature was 30 degrees.

Eventually, however, Morton Thiokol senior vice-president Jerald Mason declared that 'We have to make a management decision.' He and three other Thiokol vice-presidents, approved the launch.

But Allan McDonald, director of Thiokol's engineers after 'heated exchanges' with NASA officials, refused to sign an official approval to proceed. 'I argued before, and I argued after,' he told reporters.

**Below:** *Plumes of smoke follow segments of the space shuttle which hurtled rocket debris to earth in several directions.*

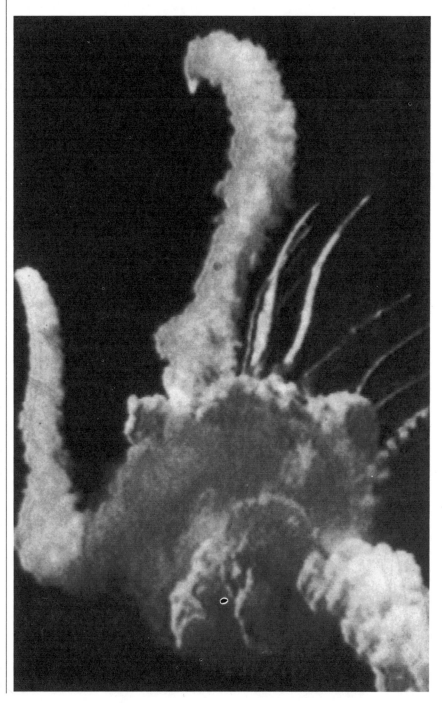

NASA, it seemed, was not interested in 'fears', but instead demanded proof that the launch would be unsafe. At one point, a NASA official supposedly asked the engineers: 'My God, when do you want me to launch, next April?' Finally NASA over-ruled the engineers.

---

NASA, it seems, was not interested in fears of an unsafe launch - only in proof. Tragically, they got it

---

Incredibly, on the morning of the actual launch NASA missed another chance to abort the launch. Icicles had formed on the huge tower that supports the craft on the launch pad and Space Agency officials - concerned that ice breaking off might damage the heat shield tiles - sent in the 'ice teams' to inspect the pad three times.

Information in one of the reports about abnormal 'cold spots' on the right booster rocket was somehow missed. That meant that its O-rings were subjected to far greater cold than on any previous flight.

### THE FINDINGS

At a public hearing of the Senate Subcommittee on Science, Technology and Space, Senator Ernest Hollings said of the disaster: 'At this particular juncture it seems like an avoidable accident rather than an unavoidable one.'

Later, he would charge that it was becoming 'apparent that NASA made a political decision to go ahead with [the] launch...despite strong objections.'

It was later revealed that since at least 1980 NASA had recognized that the seals between the booster sections were cause for concern.

On the first twelve shuttle flights, in four instances the O-rings had been partly burned away. Afterwards, the Space Agency began using a new type of putty to protect the joint - with the result that erosion of O-rings then occurred even more frequently.

Despite all the evidence NASA's top engineers and managers judged that this flaw was not serious enough to halt or delay shuttle flights.

The safety panel concluded that the tragedy had been caused by the 'failure of the pressure seal in the aft-field joint of the right solid-rocket motor', but noted that 'there was a serious flaw in the decision-making process'.

The panel was reluctant to assign personal blame for the tragedy, but instead outlined recommendations to ensure that such a disaster never happened again.

Its 285-page report to President Reagan urged that the shuttle's booster joints be entirely redesigned rather than just modified and that all the shuttle's critical parts be reviewed.

In addition, NASA had been eager to get the Challenger into orbit because of a series of earlier postponements to the original launch date three days before, on Saturday 25 January. First there was a dust storm at the emergency landing site in Senegal. Then, at Cape Canaveral, it rained, which could damage the heat-resistant tiles on the spacecraft. And on Monday, first a stuck bolt on an exterior-hatch handle, then 35mph winds delayed the launch until the next morning.

But the commission did not lay the blame entirely at NASA's feet. It also noted that the numbers of flights it had proposed had never been adequately funded by Washington, and that its budget had been so heavily slashed that even spare parts were running low.

### AFTERMATH

Four days later, on the Friday, America held its final farewell for the Seven. Under grey skies at the Johnson Space Center near Houston, where they had trained, some six thousand NASA employees, congressmen and relatives gathered to hear President Reagan.

*The sacrifice of your loved ones has stirred the soul of our nation, and, through the pain, our hearts have been opened to a profound truth: the future is not free...*

*Dick, Mike, Judy, El, Ron, Greg and Christa, your families and your country mourn your passing. We bid you goodbye, but we will never forget you.*

The American people certainly would not let NASA forget them. The Space

Agency, once a source of national pride, was subjected to lengthy overhauls and reviews determined to ensure, as far as modern technology and human errors would allow, that there would never again be a disaster like the *Challenger*.

The entire shuttle programme was also revamped and many changes made to the existing fleet. On 29 September 1988 there was a collective sigh of relief at the dramatically successful flight of the space shuttle *Discovery*, which marked America's return to manned space flight after a thirty-two-month break.

Not surprisingly, given their woes in the wake of the *Challenger* disaster, NASA officials treated the *Discovery* mission as if it were the test flight of a brand-new vehicle. Engineers estimated that four times as much work went into the new design as had gone into the original development in the mid-1970s.

The main engines located at the tail of the shuttle had been plagued by problems from the beginning, and during the enforced hiatus NASA made thirty-five changes to them.

---

The razzmatazz of the space shuttle should be put aside, urged the panel, in favour of more sensible scientific projects

---

NASA's engineers made 210 changes to the design of the orbiter itself and another 100 modifications to its highly sophisticated computer software.

But in the ensuing three years the shuttle programme was plagued by major and minor problems, putting increased pressure on the workload. In 1991 a panel concluded in a report to the White House that NASA should focus on new goals in the wake of budget cuts, the recession and its own ineptitude.

The report strongly suggested that the Agency should not spend funds buying another after the *Endeavor* joined the current fleet of three later that year. It concluded that another tragic and disastrous shuttle accident was highly probable by the end of the century.

Other points raised were putting research and development ahead of splashy TV space extravaganzas, and not

risking astronauts when robots can do the same job. NASA was told to cut costs and get back to more scientific missions.

The shuttle has been plagued by glitches in the early 1990s - everything from computer failures to clogged toilets. And the entire fleet was once grounded for five months by a dangerous fuel leak.

Still, experts say that the shuttle will play an integral part in the construction of the space station Freedom – the first step in America's plan to put a man on Mars before the year 2015.

**Below:** *Horror is frozen on the faces of watchers in the VIP area at Kennedy Space Center as the craft explodes 72 seconds after ignition.*

# EXXON VALDEZ
# Oil Spill Catastrophe

On 24 March 1989 the clear waters of Prince William Sound in Alaska became hideously polluted as the supertanker Exxon Valdez hit a reef. Ten million gallons of stinking black crude escaped after the accident that arrogant oil barons had said could never happen

laskan Eskimos are steeped in the traditions and beliefs of their forefathers. One of their deities is Sedna, goddess of the sea, a powerful ruler who deserved much homage to keep the ocean's harvest of seals and fish - the Eskimo lifeblood - well nurtured. The goddess is fabled for her distaste for man and his 'filth'.

### THE CAPTAIN WITH A DRINK PROBLEM

Environmental agencies and government legislation had gone to great lengths - far more than in other American states - to keep the straits, lakes and seaways fresh and beautiful. But in 1989 Sedna suffered the most heinous blow ever delivered by a mortal against a god when a ship called the *Exxon Valdez* ran aground in one of the most unpolluted stretches of water in the world.

The goddess's distaste was justified - man had committed one of the world's worst acts of pollution, spewing millions of gallons of crude oil into the sparkling, clear waters.

The 'big spill', as the locals now call it, occurred at precisely four minutes past midnight on 24 March 1989 when Captain Joseph Hazelwood, master of the supertanker *Exxon Valdez*, was absent from the bridge.

At forty-two, Captain Hazelwood, was

**Above:** *The tanker* Exxon San Francisco *is pushed by tugs up against the stricken* Valdez *as work begins to salvage the oil remaining aboard her.*

**Opposite:** *Snow-peaked mountains dwarf the* Exxon Valdez.

**Left:** *The* Exxon Valdez *spewed 10 million gallons of oil into the sea when it ran aground on a reef in Prince William Sound.*

at the peak of his career with Exxon and earned around £100,000 a year as one of its star captains. He had wealth, responsibility, respect...and a drinking problem which would lead the ship to tragedy on that chill, starlit night.

The discovery of oil in the remote state of Alaska in 1968 had been a boon to the locals, whose only other sources of income were fishing, hunting and tourism. The oil revenues had reduced state taxes, and there were good wages to be earned as the black gold continued to flow into the bellies of the supertankers.

But with oil came a change in the bucolic way of life that the locals had enjoyed cheek-by-jowl with the native Eskimos for centuries. As well as the ever-present risk of an accident, the tough world of oilmen and sailors had stripped the area of its innocent charm for ever.

The current boom in communities like Valdez, on Prince William Sound, was the result of years of bickering and bitter argument about how best to move the oil three thousand miles and more to the thirsty markets awaiting it. The companies drilling for it had examined many different options, including building a pipeline through Canada to California and the Mid-West.

Captains of the US oil industry, though, were not best pleased with the prospect of moving American resources across foreign territory. In the end the trans-Alaska companies and the federal government settled on a pipeline that brought the oil down to Valdez from the permafrost fields further north.

---

The Valdez pipeline is a magnificent feat of engineering running for nearly eight hundred miles across the Arctic wilderness

---

That 789-mile pipeline is one of the most remarkable engineering feats in history - 101,850 sections of 48-in diameter steel pipe going through rivers and lakes and across Arctic ranges.

Once loaded on board ships like the *Exxon Valdez* it was transported to Texan or Californian ports for refining.

In the early evening of 23 March the *Exxon Valdez* was loading up with 1.26 million barrels of oil.

Captain Hazelwood, the third mate Gregory Cousins and Robert Kagan, the helmsman, were the only crewmen to leave the ship. Against all rules that forbade drinking at sea - and an Exxon regulation which prohibited the consumption of alcohol for at least four hours before a journey was started - Hazelwood and the two others went to sink some beers at the Pipeline Club. Later, eye-witnesses would report that they had seen him drink at least four beers. Hazelwood's employers knew about his previous drinking bouts and had once sent him to a drying-out clinic.

James Shiminski, an Exxon chief mate, said: 'He had a reputation for both partying ashore and on board the ship.'

In 1984 Hazelwood was convicted for drunken driving after a car crash.

A year later he underwent a twenty-eight-day stay in an alcohol addiction clinic not far from his home on Long Island, New York.

THE FATEFUL JOURNEY BEGINS

Within an hour of his latest drinking session Hazelwood and his party had returned to the dockside ready to board the vessel for sailing.

At 9.10pm he was on the bridge of the *Exxon Valdez* as she slipped her moorings for Long Beach, California, where a substantial refinery complex would process her cargo.

William Murphy was the harbour pilot who was obliged by law to navigate the ship for the two hours it took to weave through the shallow sea lane littered with jagged rocks. Later he would tell investigators that he smelled alcohol on the skipper's breath that night but that his demeanour did not indicate that he was intoxicated.

The ship, bigger than three football pitches end to end, lumbered off into the still, freezing night an hour before her scheduled sailing time. In the bowels of the ship engines capable of producing over 35,000 horsepower pushed her on her way.

Shortly after 11.30pm, only minutes after the pilot Murphy had left the bridge and returned home on a harbour launch, Hazelwood radioed the local coastguard and said he was altering the course of the ship from the outward, ice-infested channel to the inbound, ice-free channel.

At approximately 11.50pm Hazelwood turned over the bridge, and therefore control of the ship, to the third mate, Cousins. The second mate, Lloyd LeCaine, was in a deep sleep.

Regulations stated that it was LeCaine who should have assumed the responsibility. However, maritime experts have since concurred it was a rule more often broken than observed by many skippers.

The coastguard had to give permission for the turn into the inbound channel - which it did - but shortly afterwards lost radar contact with the ship. Hazelwood had told Cousins to make a right turn back into the outbound channel when the vessel reached a navigational point near Busby Island, three miles north of a jagged underwater outcrop of rock called Bligh Reef.

The captain was just fifteen feet away from the bridge, completing paperwork in his cabin, when disaster struck. The *Exxon Valdez* was more than a mile from where she should have been.

One reason could have been that helmsman Robert Kagan, feeling that the ship was turning too sharply back towards the outbound channel, used a counter-rudder manoeuvre to slow the swing. Such a measure was logged in the ship's course recorder, a kind of maritime 'black box'.

---

**Captain Hazelwood heard the groaning of tortured steel beneath him**

---

Cousins repeated the order for a hard-right rudder, and then Captain Hazelwood felt the groaning and twisting of steel underneath him and knew that something had gone terribly, terribly wrong. Then came the phone call from Cousins: 'We are in trouble!'

Hazelwood bolted to the bridge and knew instantly from the lack of motion that the ship had grounded on the reef and was hanging precariously like a gigantic see-saw. His first job was to make sure it didn't slip off the reef, which could cause her either to keel over or to break her back. Hazelwood was in for the longest night of his life.

Beneath his 987-ft-long ship were huge rents in her steel hull, some fifteen feet long. Eight of the fifteen cargo holds were ruptured, and in time some 240,000 barrels of oil, forty-two gallons in each,

**Below:** *The* Valdez *caused an environmental disaster ecologists had been warning about for 15 years - and which oil companies said was 'impossible'.*

would be released into the sound with catastrophic effect.

Despite some question marks over Hazelwood's sobriety or otherwise, investigators would later say he showed excellent seamanship in his efforts at damage limitation. By adjusting the engine power he was able to keep the vessel firmly pressed up against the reef and stable.

Once the *Exxon Valdez* had run aground she was picked up again by the coastguard radar. In what seems to have been a case of bureaucratic bungling, the coastguards did not board the stricken ship until three hours later.

### THE BUNGLED CLEAN-UP

Daylight brought with it full realization of the environmental horror that had occurred. Already the carcasses of sea otters and birds had begun to be seen on the outer reaches of the spill.

---

First the coastguards lost touch with the ship on their radar, then it took them three hours to reach her after she grounded

---

The scene was the environmental disaster that protesters had been warning of for years. But two years before the disaster the consortium of powerful oil companies had said haughtily: 'It is highly unlikely that there will ever be a spill of any magnitude.'

The consortium further boasted that slick-fighting materials would be on hand within five hours to neutralize the effects of any spill.

But the first clean-up crews did not get to the spill site until ten hours afterwards, during which time the 10 million-plus gallons gurgling from the shattered hull of the *Exxon Valdez* continued unabated into the sound. And even then they were pitifully inadequately equipped to deal with a spillage of such major proportions.

They had been lulled into complacency even though their equipment had been proved taxed to the limit in dealing with a small spill of just 1500 barrels in January the same year. There were no

*Below: One of the several oil cargo tanks aboard the 987-foot Valdez. Workers removed 1600 tons of damaged steel from the ship's hull before putting her back in service.*

booms to contain the spreading slick and few skimmers, which swept the surface of the water collecting oil.

---

All the equipment to deal with the vast slick was inadequate or out of action

---

The slick was still spreading, but chemicals could not be used because the water was calm, which rendered them ineffective. The coastguard, which by law was supposed to have vessels on hand capable of dealing with a 'major' spill, had its minuscule fleet of ships two thousand miles away in San Francisco.

By Sunday, 26 March, winds had picked up across the sound and were whipping the surface oil into a 'mousse' - a frothy cream that defied attempts to skim it up. Attempts were made to burn it, also to no avail.

The oil had now formed the biggest slick in history – covering 900 square miles, fouling the inlets that are home to sea otters, the nesting shallows of dozens of bird species and the once-pristine beaches where seals suckled their young.

At the last count the body count was grim: 86,000 birds, among them 139 rare bald eagles, 984 sea otters, 25,000 fish, 200 seals and several dozen beavers were the victims. Millions of mussels, sea urchins and other forms of marine life were wiped out for ever. Thousands more sea otters are feared to be dead, their bodies weighted down with oil to sink for ever beneath the surface.

---

**Some beaches had to be treated with detergent chemicals seven times**

---

Some beaches had to be treated seven times with detergents and other chemicals. Environmental scientist Paul Willard said:

*The spill happened in almost the worst place possible. The jagged coast of Prince William Sound is dotted with innumerable coves and inlets where the spilled oil collected and stayed for months, killing young fish that spawn in the shallows.*

### LAWSUITS

Exxon came under a barrage of criticism. Newspaper advertisements urged people not to buy Exxon products and their service stations were deserted, the result of national disgust at their seemingly cavalier treatment of the disaster.

Exxon's President, Frank Iarossi, countered with the pledge of a billion dollars for the clean-up. Exxon also made a commitment to compensate fishermen and others who had directly suffered because of the spill.

In apportioning blame for the big spill it has been all too easy merely to point the finger at Captain Hazelwood and his

love for a drink too many. He was fired almost immediately after the disaster. Exxon cited as their reason positive blood alcohol tests taken nine hours after the ship grounded. But subsequent inquiries have concluded that he acted honourably afterwards and with great skill, and that he may only have gone over the limit afterwards when he needed to steady his nerves.

The fatigue of his crew, as much as the combination of errors in navigation that night, may well have played a part in the grounding of the *Exxon Valdez*. There were just twenty crewmen working that night on board one of the biggest vessels afloat - a reduction of twenty-four from when Hazelwood had first sailed in her.

Also at fault were the coastguards who, had they not lost the ship on their radar, might well have been able to notify her that she was navigating into dangerous waters.

New, more stringent alcohol rules have been applied in the disaster's wake, and double-hulled vessels are replacing single-hulled ones operating in the sound. But for those who live there, and for the defiled goddess Sedna, it is all a matter of too little, too late.

**Above:** *Oil from the stricken tanker is pumped aboard its sister ship the* **Exxon Baton Rouge** *as clean-up efforts continued on the oil spill in Prince William Sound.*

# SAN FRANCISCO
# Rocked by Earthquakes

# Perched astride the San Andreas Fault, San Francisco has suffered two horrific earthquakes this century. But the Big One, the one that will utterly destroy this beautiful city, is still to come - and that fate is inevitable

**Opposite:** *The smouldering rubble of an apartment building in San Francisco's Marina district after the 1989 earthquake struck.*

**Below:** *The devastated main shopping centre, with famous Telegraph Hill in the background, in 1906.*

**Bottom:** *Crowds watch part of old San Francisco go up in smoke.*

Tony Bennett left his heart in it, Al Jolson begged it to 'open up that Golden Gate', and a generation of hippies were urged to put flowers in their hair when they visited it.

San Francisco's splendid vistas and its old European-style houses and plazas, serviced by a quaint cable-car network from another age, combine to make the city by the bay one of the most splendid and 'livable' of all the great American metropolises. In art, culture and social tolerance - it is home to America's biggest gay community as well as the nation's most rapidly expanding Asian and Japanese districts - San Francisco stands out.

Only one force - a massive, irresistible force - stands in the way of the Utopia which San Francisco has become for so many people. And that force is nature.

## A CATASTROPHE BOUND TO HAPPEN

Twice this century - in 1906 and in 1989 - nature has flexed its considerable muscles to prove itself more powerful than the most reinforced of reinforced concrete, not to mention the strongest of tungsten steel.

But the two earthquakes which wrought havoc on San Francisco are only the precursors of the the ultimate Big

One - the one which will level this beautiful man-made monument. This is not a Nostradamus-type prediction; the city's location dictates that one day it will crumble, burn and disappear into great fissures, to linger only as a memory.

---

Imagine two badly stacked dinner plates with a delicate wineglass on top - the wineglass is San Francisco

---

The reason for the city's ultimate demise lies in a mammoth geological hiccup spawned in the days when the earth itself was formed. Called the San Andreas Fault, it is literally a 650-mile-long crack in the earth where the Pacific plate is slowly but surely sliding underneath the landmass of California, itself part of the North America plate.

Scientists say one way for the human mind to grasp what is happening is to put two dinner plates on top of one another and move them so they overlap at each side. Place a full wine glass on the top plate and move the bottom one. Slow movements will cause the wine to shake - more energetic ones to make it spill over the top. The most violent wrench of all will see the glass and contents topple, spill and smash. That is the fate that awaits San Francisco.

This is not to scaremonger - the Big One could come next year or in a thousand years' time. All that is certain is that it will eventually come.

### REHEARSAL

The first massive quake to devastate San Francisco occurred on 18 April 1906. When the first shock waves were felt the natives of the gold rush town that grew into the West Coast's most thriving community were blasé about it. Tremors happened a lot there - still do, in fact - and it was not uncommon to feel a rumbling beneath your feet or to watch the table cruet dance before your eyes.

Indeed, on that fateful day, when the newspaper magnate William Randolph Hearst was awakened in his ornate New York apartment to be told that his beloved native San Francisco was being consumed by earthquake and fire, he

**Above:** *A 1906 photograph of the corner of South Market Street and Main Street.*

**Right:** *Helpers set up an open-air canteen amid the devastation of San Francisco.*

replied: 'Don't overplay it - they often have earthquakes over in California.'

The San Francisco earthquake was sadly everything, and more, that his minion had told him - the single most cataclysmic event of the age.

---

'Don't overplay it,' said William Randolph Hearst, when first informed of the 1906 quake

---

The quake is estimated to have registered 8.3 on the Richter scale, the yardstick for seismic measurements, although it was only an estimate as the measurement system had not been devised then. That force is greater than thirty nuclear underground blasts triggered simultaneously. Eight hundred people perished in the collapsing buildings and the chasms which opened up in the streets, or in the firestorm which swiftly consumed the wooden buildings in the aftermath of the vibrations.

Mary Monti, now ninety-four, recalled the events of that grim day.

*It knocked me out of bed. The walls of the house we lived in shook and then cracked - great spider's web cracks as the plaster crumbled with the force. We ran into the street and the surface of the road was boiling and rolling. My mother grabbed us kids and we got out of town on a cart, into the hills. Everywhere there was fire. Suddenly a new fire would start up as gas mains got ruptured or kerosene was spilled.*

She was one of three hundred thousand people made homeless by the devastating natural disaster which destroyed close to twenty-nine thousand buildings.

---

On Telegraph Hill Italian families tried to douse the flames with ten thousand gallons of wine

---

The quake had destroyed water lines as well as gas pipes, so firemen could not tackle the blazes. On Telegraph Hill, one of the more celebrated promontories in the city, Italian immigrant families wasted ten thousand gallons of wine which they poured on to the flames.

Packs of looters roamed the streets, robbing shattered stores and stealing from the dead who lined the gutters. And from the few remaining lampstands hung those robbers who were caught by tearful and vengeful citizens.

The author, Jack London, wrote a moving account of the disaster for Collier's weekly magazine:*San Francisco is gone!...On Wednesday morning at a quarter past five came the earthquake. A minute later the flames were leaping upward. In a dozen different quarters south of Market Street, in the working class ghetto, and in the factories, fire started. There was no opposing the flames. There was no organization, no communication...all the shrewd contrivances and safeguards of man had been thrown out of gear by thirty seconds twitching of the earth's crust.*

By the time the fires burned out more than 75 per cent of San Francisco was destroyed, four hundred city blocks in ruins. It provoked scientists and government to pour money into researching the massive fault and what could be done to predict the next quake.

### EARTHQUAKE TECHNOLOGY

At the time of the earthquake, geologists had only a sketchy understanding of the processes that combine to move and shake the earth. They realized that the disaster was linked to the San Andreas Fault, and that the land to the west of the faultline was edging northwards.

A geologist from Pennsylvania, Harry Fielding Reid, observing twisted fence posts and shattered roadways, found that there had been a ground lurch of as much as 21 feet during the quake.

More importantly, he recognized that the great blocks of earth on either side of the faultline had been under tremendous strain long before the earthquake happened. Tremendous friction had caused two faces of the fault to stick until

*Below: A rare, early photograph of one of the pioneers who founded San Francisco in 1849.*

Above: *A dramatic photograph of San Francisco's ruined skyline after the earthquake and ensuing fire storm swept the city in 1906.*

the accumulating forces were at last released with a massive snap.

In the 1970s scientists recognized that different sections along the San Andreas Fault were moving at different rates, causing strain to build up in some areas more than others. From Point Arena to San Juan Bautista, a small town south of San Francisco, and from Parkfield down to the Mexican border, the fault is stuck.

When the tremendous force has built up and the fault moves - then the next earthquake is born. California quake expert William Bakun says:

*First and foremost we want to learn the earthquake generation process. Then we want to learn how to predict them in areas where they are a hazard.*

Sadly, it is still not an exact science, although the colleges and universities of California lead the world in earthquake technology. Another quake expert, David Langston, said:

*All we can do is to keep on trying to predict and hope we improve sufficiently to give the population a fair warning when a huge quake is on its way and not be accused of crying wolf.*

Following hard on those studies, in 1980 the Federal Emergency Management Agency worked out a scenario that earthquakes would strike at both San Francisco and Los Angeles. Their findings were grim, with death predictions topping fifty thousand in the San Francisco quake and property

damage at over $20 million. The worst case scenario says that in the quake's wake will be a wasteland of fires and looting, with possible disease rife in the breakdown of law and order.

In 1989 a TV-age disaster dramatically set the scene for what will one day befall the city on a much larger scale.

## FURTHER WARNING

In the words of housewife Annette Henry, who was in one of the city's main thoroughfares when it struck, here is what the great quake of October 1989 felt like: 'It was as if God just clapped his hands. The ground was like a wave underneath a surfboard, and the cars on the highway were jumping up and down like in a Disney movie. Every time we have an earthquake in California we giggle, we're cool, we're blasé about it. This time was different. I was just hanging on thinking, it's not so funny any more. I thought we were having the Big One.'

---

'The cars on the highway were jumping up and down like a Disney movie'

---

Rocks in the San Andreas Fault couldn't stand the pressure any longer and 58,000-foot-thick blocks of the earth's crust heaved violently. Pressure waves, travelling at five miles per second, raced from the quake's epicentre,

south-east of San Francisco through the bedrock under the Santa Cruz Mountains.

It hit San Francisco during the evening rush hour of Tuesday, 17 October and within fifteen seconds had reduced many buildings to rubble, had destroyed a section of the Bay Bridge, collapsed over a mile of elevated highway, and left the historic Marina district engulfed by fire.

Thanks to global TV coverage of the World Series baseball game between the Oakland A's and San Francisco Giants, viewers as far away as London witnessed the first shocks as the Candlestick Park stadium visibly swayed and huge cracks appeared in the concrete walls.

Most of the hundred deaths from the earthquake occurred when a mile-long section of Interstate 880, an elevated freeway, collapsed on to the lower roadway. Dozens of people were trapped in their cars that were concertinaed together by tons of reinforced concrete.

'It just sandwiched in,' said Henry Reniera, manager for emergency services for Oakland.

*It is like a war zone out there. The upper deck fell like a hammer blow on to the lower deck, showering motorists below with rubble and cars. Trapped victims beneath tons of debris have been frantically honking their horns and we are rushing in massive amounts of lifting equipment and hydraulic jacks in a bid to get to them. It is an eerie sound, muffled horns that slowly fade as the car batteries run flat and you know that humans are trapped in there.*

The most moving rescue of the entire disaster occurred in the rubble beneath the collapsed Nimitz Freeway section. Patrick Wallace, a paper mill worker, was one of the first on the scene to the sandwiched cars and heard the terrified screams of children trapped in a red car. Together with other rescuers he was able to help free an eight-year-old girl, Cathy Berumen, but her six-year-old brother Julio was trapped - pinned in the wreckage by the body of his dead mother.

Risking his life from further after-shocks, Dr Dan Allen crawled through a three-foot gap to give sedatives to Julio until another doctor, a childcare specialist, could climb up a fire truck's ladders.

Dr Thomas Betts said: 'Nothing could have prepared me for what I saw there. The boy was in shock. He would just cry and run his hands over his mother's face.'

After two hours of frantic work the medical team were no nearer to getting Julio free. His right leg was crushed beyond repair and they needed to get him out for immediate treatment. The boy was put under sedation while a chainsaw was deployed to cut his mother in half before his own leg was amputated.

As fires blazed through the night, glass popped from the twisted skyscrapers built without earthquake specifications and the sirens wailed eerily across the city, the politicians and planners did have some

cause for comfort. Initial reports proved that the destruction was intensely localized, concentrated in older structures that had not been upgraded to withstand earthquakes. The collapsed highway section, which claimed most lives, was itself thirty years old.

Experts concurred that the strict Californian building code - instituted after the 1906 disaster in a bid to minimize damage in future quakes and updated in the late eighties to incorporate the lessons learned from the 1971 San Fernando and 1985 Mexico City quakes - played a large part in minimizing the damage.

But there is no denying the inevitability of the scale of disaster if a new quake hits the 8.3 Richter scale reading of the 1906 one. A study made by the National Oceanic and Atmospheric Administration after the quake concluded that forty times as much energy would be released as in the 1989 one, resulting in thousands upon thousands of deaths.

San Franciscans are still clearing up the mess of the quake, a process which will

**Above:** *San Francisco's elegant, wooden houses burn after the 1989 quake.*

**Below:** *This scene of devastation was once a six-lane highway. It was reduced to twisted metal and shattered concrete.*

take the best part of ten years to complete. They are proud of having come through, and flaunt their fatalistic attitude to nature's aggression. The columnist for the *San Francisco Chronicle*, Herb Caen, summed up the city by the bay when he wrote in the days after the quake: 'We live with earthquakes and we live on a fault and we live dangerously. And it's exciting.'

# MYSTERIES

# TUTANKHAMUN
## Curse of the Boy King

Those who 'defile' the tomb of the Egyptian boy king Tutankhamun have suffered misfortune, disease and sudden death. Are they the victims of a three thousand-year-old curse?

**Above:** *Howard Carter stands above the excavations at the tomb of Tutankhamun in 1923.*

**Right:** *Archaeologists discuss their findings during the excavations.*

**Opposite:** *Howard Carter kneels before the wonder of Tutankhamun's yellow quartzite sarcophagus.*

**Below:** *Howard Carter leaves the White House after a meeting with President Calvin Coolidge in 1929.*

**W**ith trepidation among the watching throng, the tomb of the Egyptian pharaoh Tutankhamun was reopened in the summer of 1991 after being closed for nine months because of a growth of fungus within the ancient vault. As research work was resumed on the tomb at Luxor in southern Egypt, the world wondered whether the amazing seventy-year sequence of bad luck, sickness and death attributed to the legendary curse of the pharaoh would strike yet again.

### DREADFUL WARNINGS

The so-called Curse of Tutankhamun first fascinated the public in the early twenties as plans were laid to reopen the tomb for the first time in three thousand years.

The amateur archaeologist, fifty-seven-year-old Lord Carnarvon, was well aware of the curse as he prepared to excavate the fabled, treasure-laden tomb. While still in Britain before the start of his exploration, the fanatical Egyptologist had consulted the celebrated mystic of his day, Count Hamon, who delivered to him this message: 'Lord Carnarvon not to enter tomb. Disobey at his peril. If ignored will suffer sickness. Will not recover. Death will claim him in Egypt.'

Carnarvon, however, was intent on continuing the biggest and costliest expedition of his lifetime. His team had worked on the project for years, ever since being granted a concession to excavate the most heavily dug site in the whole of Egypt - the Valley of the Kings.

The Earl and his American partner Howard Carter started digging in earnest only in 1917. But during five disappointing seasons they discovered only some alabaster jars inscribed with the names of Rameses II and Meremptah.

The partners debated whether to attempt a sixth season's dig...and decided to give the project one last try.

### THE TOMB OF THE BOY KING

The one area on the site where Carnarvon and Carter had not attempted a dig was so churned up by past excavations that no one had thought it worthwhile to investigate further. The partners ordered the removal of some disused huts.

Carnarvon had returned to England when the first hut was demolished - to reveal beneath it a step cut into the rock. Carnarvon was telephoned, and the excited peer persuaded Carter to reseal the site while he made the three-week journey back to Egypt.

The two explorers now embarked on the most nerve-racking week of their lives. By now it was clear that the greatest archaeological discovery of the century was within their grasp...the revelation of the tomb of an obscure, adolescent pharaoh, untouched from the day when his frail body had been sealed up by the slaves of ancient Egypt.

The awe and superstition surrounding the find caused its own problems. As they neared their golden goal, the Westerners had difficulty keeping their team together as waves of fear swept through the native diggers.

The sense of dread was heightened when an inscription above the entrance to the tomb was translated. It read ominously: 'Death will come to those who disturb the sleep of the pharaohs.'

The breakthrough came on 17 February 1923, when the archaeologists entered the funerary chamber of the boy king. Carter exclaimed: 'Things, wonderful things!' as he gazed in awe at the sumptuous treasures.

---

'Things, wonderful things!' exclaimed Carter as he gazed in awe at the rich treasure around him

---

In an antechamber were golden boxes and caskets, golden chairs, a golden throne, golden couches, statues, animal heads, alabaster vases and a golden snake. A further chamber was opened and, when a torch was shone through, the archaeologists reported what appeared to be a wall of gold.

Three doors led from this shrine. Two were bolted and sealed, and these the explorers left for the moment. Instead they unblocked a small passageway which opened up another chamber of treasures, all in gold, depicting gods and goddesses and visions of the afterlife.

Still to be discovered was what lay

*Below: The boy king's tomb with the hills of the Valley of the Kings in the background.*

*Bottom: A later photograph of the excavation and the Valley of the Kings. The tent is the 'police headquarters'.*

behind one of the two remaining sealed doors - the solid gold coffin containing the mummified body of young King Tutankhamun. That revelation of ancient splendour beyond belief was yet to come.

### THE CURSE STRIKES

Opening the tomb had uncovered ancient riches beyond belief. But it had also released a mysterious, dark force that had lain dormant for three thousand years.

Two months later Carnarvon was dead. He had taken to his bed at Cairo's Hotel Continental, complaining: 'I feel like hell.' His son cared for him in his last hours, the archaeologist's body racked

*Above: **A local helper emerging from the tomb bearing the statuette believed to be of Tutankhamun's queen, a daughter of the earlier pharoah Akhenaton.***

*Below: **Howard Carter, assisted by two local helpers, uses pillows to protect the gilded sidepieces of Tutankhamun's royal coach. A seated Lord Carnarvon looks on.***

with the poison and fever from a mosquito bite.

As he passed away, the lights of the city mysteriously flashed on and off. And back home at his country house in England, a dog howled pitifully in the middle of the night. It awoke the entire household before, gasping for breath, the animal lay down and expired.

It was not until the winter of 1925 that Carter could resume his work, entering first one and then the second of the final sealed and bolted doors leading to the sarcophagus. What was revealed to Carter is described in his own words.

---

The ancient Eqyptian builders had carefully numbered each of eighty component parts of the shrine

---

*With intense excitement I drew back the bolts of the last and unsealed doors. They slowly swung open and there, filling the entire area within...stood an immense yellow quartzite sarcophagus. Specially striking were the outstretched hand and wing of the goddess sculptured on the lid as if to ward off an intruder.*

The lid of the sarcophagus weighed more than half a ton, and there was a further delay as hoists were called in to raise it. The shrines had to be dismantled and removed, a task made easier by the fact that their eighty component parts had

all been carefully numbered by the original builders.

When the lifting gear took the strain and gently raised the lid of the coffin, all that could be seen was a bundle of rotting linen cloth. But beneath was a golden effigy of Tutankhamun on the lid of a coffin - the famous effigy glitteringly restored and photographed and now known around the world.

No wonder Howard Carter's descriptions of his discovery were so euphoric. But his words were soon overshadowed by the astonishing catalogue of tragedy that followed the disturbance of the pharaoh's remains.

For it was not only Lord Carnarvon who met his premature fate soon after entering the outer shrine of King Tutankhamun. Fellow archaeologist Arthur Mace, who had been there when the tomb was opened, died shortly afterwards. He too was taken ill at the Hotel Continental, complaining of extreme fatigue.

A close friend of Carnarvon's, George Gould, travelled to Egypt to pay his last respects. He collapsed with a fever just hours after taking a look at the tomb. Radiologist Archibald Reid, whose equipment was used to determine the age of the tomb, was sent back to England complaining of fatigue. He died soon after disembarking.

Six years after revealing Tutankhamun, twelve of those who had witnessed the opening of the tomb had died. And the curse continued to take its toll.

*Above: **Tourists hunt for souvenirs in the Valley of the Kings.***

*Below: **The closing of the tomb of King Tutankhamun following a dispute between Howard Carter and the Egyptian government.***

Within a decade only two of the original excavation team survived, and about twenty-five others connected with the expedition had died unexpectedly. For a while the curse seemed content with the victims it had claimed.

### ...AND STRIKES AGAIN

Then in 1966, on the eve of an international exhibition of the relics, Egypt's director of antiquities, Mohammed Ibrahim, begged that the treasures should be kept in the country. He had dreamed of death should they go on their planned trip to Paris. He was over-ruled. Leaving a final meeting in Cairo, Ibrahim was hit by a car and died instantly.

---

Only six years after the opening of Tutankhamun's tomb, twelve of those present had died

---

The fear was revived in 1972 when the golden death mask of King Tutankhamun was being sent to London for an exhibition. Dr Gamal Mehrez, successor to the dead Mohammed Ibrahim, was in charge of the despatch from Cairo.

Dr Mehrez had no fears of any curse, saying: 'I, more than anyone else in the world, have been involved in the tombs and mummies of the pharaohs. Yet I am still alive. I am the living proof that all the tragedies linked to the pharaohs were pure coincidence.'

Sure enough, the arrangements for the removal of King Tutankhamun's golden relics went ahead without problems. The collection was packed and loaded on to lorries to be taken to the airport.

That evening, Dr Mehrez, having overseen the end of the preparations, breathed a justified sigh of relief as he prepared to leave the Cairo museum. Moments later he slumped to the floor and died of 'circulatory collapse'.

---

Whoever scoffs at the curse seems to become its next victim

---

Strangely, of all those associated with the relics, the excavation co-leader, Howard Carter, defied the curse and died of natural causes in 1939.

There have been many theories about the Curse of King Tutankhamun. Some say poisonous substances were sealed in the tomb. An atomic scientist, Professor Louis Bulgarini, postulated that the ancient Egyptians may have used radioactive material to safeguard the sacred burial site.

He said: 'It is definitely possible that the Egyptians used atomic radiation to protect their holy places. The floors of the tombs could have been covered with

uranium or the grave could have been finished with radioactive rock.'

But most chilling of all is the theory of author Phillip Vandenburg. In his book *The Curse of the Pharaohs* he says that the pyramids and tombs were the perfect breeding ground for bacteria which created a fatal virus. It is certainly a theory that those who had the task of reopening Tutankhamun's tomb in 1991 could not forget...For the reason it was shut down was the spread of a virulent fungus, caused by bacteria from the breath of millions of visitors.

*Above: The Egyptian cabinet and their followers gather for the official reopening of the tomb after Carter's return to London.*

*Below: Sixty cases of invaluable artifacts are removed from the tomb en route for the Cairo museum.*

# CROWHURST
# Ocean-going Fraud

Drummed out of the RAF and the Army, failed as a businessman, Donald Crowhurst thought he could redeem himself with a lone voyage round the world. When his venture seemed doomed to failure he perpetrated a colossal fraud that in the end even he could not handle.

I n 1968, in the aftermath of Sir Francis Chichester's historic single-handed voyage around the globe, the conquest of the oceans caught the imagination of the world. Not since the days of Henry the Navigator or Columbus had people been so stirred by tales of tough men in ships battling against the lonely sea and the sky; not to explore new worlds, but rather to discover themselves.

As one lone sailor of the time, a romantic Frenchman, put it: 'When one has listened for months to the hum of the wind and the sea, to the language of the infinite - one is afraid of being brutally cast back into the company of people...'

**Above:** *Francis Chichester prepares to sail out of Sydney Harbour on board the famous* Gypsy Moth IV *on his voyage back to England in 1967.*

**Opposite:** *Inspired by Chichester, adventurer Donald Crowhurst decided to seek fame with a lone ocean voyage.*

**Below:** *Francis Chichester sails up the Thames, heading from Greenwich to the City of London on board* Gypsy Moth IV.

Some, with rather more faith than nautical wisdom, climbed into beer barrels or bathtubs and paddled forth to brave the elements - only to be turned back by the first loudhailer from an exasperated lifeboat skipper.

Others set sail in sleek, expensive craft, using the ultimate in twentieth-century marine technology, and were never seen again. Donald Crowhurst was one of these - but he was no maritime hero. His was one of the most bizarre voyages ever undertaken by a lone sailor.

### THE MAN WITH A CHIP ON HIS SHOULDER

In May 1967 Crowhurst was not among the crowd who stood on Plymouth Hoe and cheered Francis Chichester's return to fame, fortune and a knighthood from his round-the-world voyage in *Gypsy Moth IV*. At the age of thirty-five, Crowhurst was himself a fairly accomplished sailor. He admired Chichester and had read all his books.

What Crowhurst resented was the money that Francis Chichester was making out of his epic voyage

But, instead of driving the short distance from his home in Bridgwater, Somerset, to see the triumphant arrival of his hero, Crowhurst spent the day in a perverse fit of jealousy sailing his own small yacht in the Bristol Channel.

He told friends that he could not understand what all the fuss was about.

*Above:* **Gypsy Moth IV** *was opened to the public in a new dry dock alongside the famous clipper* **Cutty Sark** *at Greenwich in 1968. Crowhurst yearned to sail Chichester's yacht.*

What Crowhurst resented most was the money that Chichester was making out of his voyage. He was receiving sponsorship, royalties and advertising contracts from companies who wanted to attach his name to their products. Chichester was likely to become a very rich man. And Donald Crowhurst was broke.

Born in India in 1932, the son of an expatriate railway official, Crowhurst had been commissioned into the RAF as an electronics engineer. He was later asked to leave the service after several breaches of discipline.

The young Donald promptly joined the Army, was again commissioned and settled down to take a course in electronic weaponry. His new career did not last long. After a night out on the town he borrowed a car to get back to his barracks and was stopped by police. He was asked to resign his commission.

After trying his hand at various jobs, Crowhurst joined an electronics firm in Bridgwater as chief design engineer, married Clare, a charming, intelligent Irish girl, and rapidly had four children.

Still the wild ex-serviceman could not settle down. A naturally gifted scientist, Crowhurst would spend hours tinkering in his shed with electronic equipment. On days off he would sail his twenty-foot sloop *Pot of Gold* off the Devon coast.

A pot of gold was precisely what Crowhurst hoped to make by realizing his dream of starting his own business. He had designed a pistol-shaped gadget called a Navicator, a radio direction-finding device for yachtsmen.

---

After he crashed his new Jaguar and suffered head injuries Crowhurst's personality changed for the worse

---

Crowhurst persuaded his widowed mother to sell her house and lend him money to launch his new firm, which he called Electron Utilization. At first business boomed. He employed up to six people and bought a new Jaguar car, but in true Crowhurst fashion he drove it too fast and had a nasty crash in which he sustained head injuries.

He recovered, but his wife Clare claimed that his personality changed after the accident. Crowhurst, normally a mild, affable man, would fly into fits of rage or simply stare moodily out of the window.

Certainly his business suffered, and by 1967 Crowhurst had to go cap in hand to a local businessman, Stanley Best, to borrow £1000 to keep it afloat.

This, then, was Donald Crowhurst on the day Francis Chichester sailed up Plymouth Sound. A failed airman, a failed Army officer, and shortly, it seemed, to become a failed businessman.

Donald Crowhurst read the plaudits for Chichester in the following day's newspapers and decided that here was a way of gaining publicity for himself and his ailing company and at last finding that elusive pot of gold.

## A WAY OUT OF THE MESS

Within months of Chichester's return, scores of yachtsmen began working out how they could go one better. The most obvious feat would be a *non-stop* round-the-world voyage. The most obvious...but also the most daunting.

Even if they succeeded, each of them knew they would not see another human being for up to ten months. They would have to sail their tiny craft single-handedly for thirty thousand miles across every ocean of the world.

They would face all these dangers alone - yet still there were men who were desperate to make the attempt. And Donald Crowhurst was one of them.

The only problem was, he didn't have a proper boat. Nor the means with which to buy one. Certainly his own little yacht, the *Pot of Gold*, would barely make it across the English Channel, let alone around the world. And his funds were, to put it mildly, extremely low - Stanley Best was beginning to rue the day he had

**Above:** *Old man of the sea Sir Francis Chichester stands on his head for cameramen to launch his keep-fit book in London in 1969.*

been talked into investing in Crowhurst's business, and was now asking for his money back.

Crowhurst, ever the optimist, decided he knew exactly where he could find the right boat - and it had only had one careful owner.

It had been decided that *Gypsy Moth IV* would be placed in dry dock at Greenwich as a permanent memorial to Sir Francis Chichester's epic voyage. Crowhurst wrote to the town clerk of Greenwich, asking if he could borrow the boat for a year. Chichester, however, made discreet enquiries about Crowhurst among the yachting fraternity. When he discovered that hardly anyone had ever heard of him, *Gypsy Moth* was duly launched into a sea of cement and Donald Crowhurst was left without a boat.

---

Desperate for a suitable boat, Crowhurst even tried to borrow Chichester's *Gypsy Moth IV*

---

In March 1968 the *Sunday Times* decided to hold a non-stop round-the-world race for the Golden Globe trophy. Because yachtsmen would be leaving at different times and from different ports there would be two prizes: one for the fastest voyage and another for the first yacht home.

To avoid any accidents with bathtub sailors a panel of judges was set up to vet entrants. A Mr Chay Blyth applied and they could hardly turn him down - he had, after all, rowed across the Atlantic. John Ridgway, a tough ex-SAS officer who had been Blyth's rowing companion, was also a safe bet. Robin Knox-Johnston, a twenty-eight-year-old Merchant Navy officer, was again a highly experienced sailor. And when the vetting panel received an entry form from Mr Donald Crowhurst, how could they turn him down? Had he not tried, sadly in vain, to put to sea in *Gypsy Moth IV*?

Crowhurst had indeed applied to join the race. The problem was he still did not have a boat, or the money to buy one.

He solved both problems in characteristic style by persuading his long-suffering backer, Stanley Best, to lend him another £6000. He convinced

Best that it would be the shrewdest financial move he had ever made.

In a letter, Crowhurst wrote:

*On the basis of the declared entrants so far I could win both prizes. The really exciting prospect is the possibility of a trimaran... which has three hulls... being equipped with various safety mechanisms which I have designed...*

Best agreed to lend Crowhurst the money. He said later: 'My wife tells me I must have been mad. But Donald was the most impressive and convincing of men.'

With cash in the bank Crowhurst quickly found two boatbuilding firms who between them could handle a rush job. It was already early May, and according to the race rules all entrants had to set sail by 31 October.

---

In his heart of hearts Crowhurst knew he had bitten off too much, but to call it a day was too much for his ego

---

During the frantic weeks that followed, Crowhurst became increasingly frustrated as he watched first Ridgway, then Blyth and Knox-Johnston set sail. Royal Navy Commander Nigel Tetley, with the only other trimaran in the race, soon followed.

Crowhurst spent the time attending classes in radio-telegraphy. He hired an ex-Fleet Street reporter called Rodney Hallworth, who ran a news agency in Teignmouth, Devon. Hallworth arranged for Crowhurst to be adopted by the town of Teignmouth. Crowhurst's boat would be called *Teignmouth Electron*.

As the weeks passed and the boat still remained unfinished, Crowhurst's behaviour became bizarre. He would shout and swear at friends, then go into maudlin fits of depression. It was as if he had suddenly realized what he had committed himself to. But it had all gone too far. He couldn't back out now.

First the boat smashed one of her hulls trying to avoid a ferry. Then various faults showed up in the *Teignmouth Electron*: bolts and screws would come loose at certain speeds.

Over the next few days Crowhurst became more and more distracted, and it was soon obvious to local seafarers that his voyage was doomed.

On 30 October, the night before Crowhurst was due to sail, right on the race deadline, he told his wife: 'I am not happy with the boat, she's not right. I am not prepared.' He then burst into tears.

She said later: 'I was such a fool.' She believes it was a cry for help, a last chance to abort the whole trip.

## THE START OF THE ILL-FATED VOYAGE

The following day, with the whole town of Teignmouth lining the quayside, Donald Crowhurst set sail in his untried, untested trimaran - the 9ft by 8ft cabin still littered with unopened boxes of equipment and stores.

Surprisingly, considering the haste of his departure, Crowhurst made steady progress. Within two weeks he was off Portugal, but already the *Teignmouth Electron* was revealing her faults.

Water was leaking into one of the three hulls. Worse that than, loosened screws had made the self-steering gear virtually useless. Crowhurst pirated screws from other parts of the boat to fix it.

Then disaster struck a third time. His Onan generator, the only source of electric power on the boat, failed after being drenched in seawater. It meant no lights - and no radio communication.

---

No further from home than the coast of Portugal, Crowhurst was without some of his most essential equipment

---

On Friday, 13 November, while he was still off the coast of Portugal, Crowhurst put his thoughts in writing:

*This may look like a load of excuses for stopping. That's not what I want to do. If I stop I'll disappoint a lot of people - Stanley Best most importantly...and then my family.*

And then he decided:

*I will continue south and try to get the generator working so that I can talk to Mr Best before I commit myself to any particular course or retiring from the race. If the whole thing goes quite sour: Electron Utilization bankrupt... ten years of work and worry down the drain, I would have Clare and the children still...*

By this time, Crowhurst had covered

some 1300 miles but by such a tortuous route that he had only made about 800 miles of his intended course. He was hopelessly behind all the other race starters. And, with all his problems aboard the *Teignmouth Electron*, he still had 28,000 miles to go. He must have realized then that he could not possibly complete the race, let alone win. His only recourse was, in his words, to save face.

Several days later Crowhurst managed to get the generator working. He learned over the radio that Knox-Johnston was off New Zealand, and Tetley was rounding the Cape of Good Hope. Crowhurst, now off Madeira, was thousands of miles behind. He booked a call to Stanley Best.

According to his log he had planned to plead with Best that he could only retire from the race; that he would try again next year after proper preparations; that he must have one more chance. In fact he said none of these things. Everything was going well, apart from one or two technical problems, and he warned that there might be a period of radio silence because of generator trouble.

It was the first clear hint that Donald Crowhurst had planned a new route for his round-the-world trip.

### THE FACE-SAVING CON TRICK

On 10 December Crowhurst sent a telegram to Rodney Hallworth, his press agent, claiming the new speed record for a single day's sailing of 243 miles. The story appeared in all the national papers the following day. There was, of course, no way of checking it.

No one could possibly know that back on the *Teignmouth Electron* Crowhurst was now filling in two logbooks. One showed his real course and position, which every seaman must do to help with navigation. The other consisted of the route he would show the race judges when he returned in triumph.

While the rest of the world believed that *Teignmouth Electron* was churning through the white horses of the Roaring Forties, Crowhurst was drifting aimlessly in the South Atlantic, making sure that he kept well away from passing ships.

He was killing time, waiting for the moment - months hence - when he could announce to the world that he had sailed the globe, rounded the Horn and was on his way home.

---

**After cabling about generator trouble he started to fill in two logbooks, one genuine, the other fake**

---

By the end of January, when he was officially reckoned to be somewhere in the Indian Ocean, Crowhurst realized he would have to repair his damaged third hull, otherwise he would sink. He did not have the proper equipment to do it on board, and he began to sail slowly towards the coast of Argentina.

He figured that if he landed at some remote spot on the South American coast it was unlikely that anyone would recognize him or remember who he was.

**Below:** *Donald Crowhurst poses with his wife Clare and their children Rachel, 6, Simon, 9, Roger, 8, and James, 11, before his ill-fated voyage.*

Above: *Royal Navy Commander Nigel Tetley with his wife Eve. Tetley set sail on the epic voyage shortly before an impatient Donald Crowhurst.*

For several days Crowhurst meandered around the Argentine coast, just out of sight of shore, and pored over a book called *The South American Pilot* which listed all the possible landing places.

After much indecision he picked his spot - Rio Salado, which according to his book consisted merely of a group of sheds and buildings. He landed his battered craft there on 6 March.

He was in luck. The tiny fishing village was a hundred miles from nowhere and had no telephone. The easy-going coastguard, while mentioning the visit of an eccentric English sailor in his log, did not think the incident worth reporting. Crowhurst spent several days stocking up with supplies and repairing his boat, then set sail again.

Maintaining strict radio silence - under the guise of his broken generator - Crowhurst spent the next month sailing aimlessly around the Falkland Islands. He had worked out that the earliest possible date he could reveal his position would be 15 April.

What of the other race yachtsmen? On 6 April, Robin Knox-Johnston was spotted by a passing tanker in the South Atlantic on his way home. He was now favourite to win the Golden Globe. The only other yachtsman left in the race, Commander Tetley, was reported homeward-bound 150 miles from the Falklands...where Donald Crowhurst was lurking in *Teignmouth Electron*.

Back home, Crowhurst's press agent Hallworth was having a worrying time. He had not heard from his protege for nearly three months. There had been no sightings. And he could only assume that Crowhurst was somewhere near Australia or at the bottom of the Pacific.

Then, on 9 April, Crowhurst decided to test the water. He was still not sure if his stopover in Rio Salado had been reported. He sent a cable, via Buenos Aires, which said simply: DEVON-NEWS EXETER HEADING DIGGER RAMREZ LOG KAPUT 17697 WHATS NEW OCEANBASHINGWISE.

It was a masterpiece of non-information. But Hallworth pounced upon the message. Digger Ramrez he took to mean the tiny island of Diego Ramırez, south-west of Cape Horn.

No one could raise Crowhurst to confirm his position, but these sparse details were enough for Hallworth. He filed a story to all the national papers that his boy was rounding the Horn and was on target for the fastest time. Donald Crowhurst was back in the race.

On 30 April he reached the spot he had planned and broke his radio silence with a cable congratulating Knox-Johnston on being the first man home. Now he was racing Nigel Tetley for the prize for the fastest time. But Crowhurst, alone in his cabin, had worked it all out. He did not want to win.

THE FINAL DECEPTION

By now he had realized that his fake log - with details of non-existent storms in the Indian Ocean and phoney squalls in the Pacific - would not stand up to the judges' scrutiny. If, however, he came in a close second to Tetley he would be hailed as a hero anyway. And, more importantly, he would not have to present his log to the race organizers.

Crowhurst deliberately dawdled as he headed home up the Atlantic. But Tetley had been told that *Teignmouth Electron* was hard on his heels, and pushed his already-battered boat to the limit. Off the Azores he hit a storm and sank.

It was the final dilemma. He couldn't lose - he was already two months ahead of Knox-Johnston's time. He couldn't win. The judges would spot his fraud.

He sent a telegram commiserating with Tetley, who had been rescued in his rubber dinghy. Then Donald Crowhurst, failed serviceman, failed businessman and now a failed round-the-world yachtsman, simply stopped sailing.

Ironically his radio really did break

**Below: *Renowned yachtsman Robin Knox-Johnston fights the wind and waves with his yacht* Suhaili *towards the end of the race.***

down, and he wrote in his log that he was desperate to talk to his wife Clare. He could still receive messages, however, and it must have added to his sense of impending doom when he was cabled by Hallworth that Teignmouth was putting out the flags for his homecoming.

---

**As one by one his rivals dropped out Crowhurst was faced with a terrible dilemma - if he won, his fraud would be exposed**

---

By 22 June Crowhurst had drifted into the eerie stillness of the plankton-green Sargasso Sea. He had managed to get his radio working and sent off routine messages to Hallworth, his wife and the BBC. Then, within twenty-four hours, Crowhurst went mad.

Over the next few days he wrote twelve thousand words of gibberish about the cosmos, the mind and mathematics.

The log entry finished at 11.20am on 1 July. No one will ever know exactly what happened then, but it is widely believed that Donald Crowhurst, insane with guilt, remorse and loneliness, climbed up on deck, walked to the rail and plunged into the calm Sargasso Sea.

Nine days later the *Teignmouth Electron* was spotted by a Royal Navy vessel, the *Picardy*. The trimaran was deserted, and in the cabin lay Crowhurst's damning logbooks.

When the news broke, the nation mourned the loss of one of its bravest sons of the sea. A fund was set up to help the Crowhurst family, and Knox-Johnston donated his £5000 Golden Globe prize. It was not until the logbooks were examined back in England that Crowhurst's amazing fraud was exposed.

To this day there are some who believe that Donald Crowhurst secretly made a raft from flotsam gathered from the Sargasso Sea and set sail for the nearest landfall, the Cape Verde Islands. For many years afterwards his wife did not believe her husband was dead.

Over the years there have been alleged sightings of him in the Azores and the Canary Islands. Certainly it would be ironic that Captain Conman Donald Crowhurst even cheated his own death.

# ROBIN HOOD
## Prince of Thieves?

The hero of the greenwood, who robbed the rich to pay the poor - or a murderous brigand idealized by later generations? What's the real truth about the romantic, swashbuckling figure known as Robin Hood?

*Left: Life in the green wood - subsisting by illegal hunting of the king's deer.*

Six hundred years after his death, a footnote in history was written about a small-time crook who roamed woodlands in central England.

This villain of the piece hardly warranted a mention in chronicles of the time; his exploits were less than dramatic in such a violent age. And his story would, understandably, have gone untold in a period when wars, plague and famine were not uncommon.

But for some unfathomable reason, the legend of this crook has been writ large in history. His name, all these centuries after his death, is better known today than it was when he was alive. The name ... Robin Hood.

### DEBUNKING THE MYTH

In March 1988 the town council of Nottingham in the East Midlands issued a report on the most famous inhabitant of their city. Since over the years they had received thousands of requests for information about Robin and his Merry Men, the council decided to issue the definitive statement on the matter.

Extraordinarily for a place that owed its repute to the ages-old story, the councillors took it upon themselves to cast some doubt on the veracity of the legend of the elusive Master Hood.

According to Nottingham's assiduous researchers, the dashing hero who robbed the rich to help the poor never even met his paramour, Maid Marian. Friar Tuck, they said, was a myth. Little John was grumpy and short-tempered - nothing like the happy-go-lucky character of folklore. Their survey went on in this vein...

But when the town councillors debunked the legend that was one of their few claims to fame, they found that they were only the latest in a long line of cynics. For when examining the history of Robin Hood, it is almost impossible to separate fact from fiction. Many before them had researched this fascinating story - and still the ghost of Robin Hood has not been laid to rest.

So what is the myth and magic of the lad in Lincoln green whose daring exploits still thrill to this day, in books and films and on television? One can accept what serious researchers have unearthed - that Robin plundered from travellers riding the Great North Road near Barnsdale in South Yorkshire, and that he forayed with his outlaw band thirty miles away in Sherwood Forest. Or one can accept the romantic version that this handsome hero really did rob from the rich only to give to the poor.

### THE HISTORICAL FACTS

Robin's minor rule of the English 'badlands' reputedly occurred around 1261. But the first mention of him did not come until a century later when he was briefly referred to by the Scottish

*Opposite: The Robin Hood statue in the city of Nottingham.*

*Below: Design for a stage costume of Robin Hood from 1904.*

historian Fordun, who died in 1386. Further written word of his exploits came in the sixteenth century.

According to the chronicler John Stow, he was an outlaw in the reign of Richard I. He supported a hundred men, all tall and good archers, with the spoils he took, yet he 'suffered no woman to be oppressed or otherwise molested. Poor men's goods he spared, abundantlie relieving them with which by theft he got from abbeys and houses of rich earles.'

Let's start by taking the most charitable view of his history. The tale must begin with records which show that a Robin Hood did exist - in Wakefield, Yorkshire, in the thirteenth and fourteenth centuries.

This character is documented as being born in 1290 and christened Robert Hood. The family surname is spelt three ways in the old court records: Hod, Hode and Hood. But it is clearly stated that Robin's father was a retainer of Earl Warenne, lord of the manor of Wakefield.

So how did history's most famous petty thief launch himself on his rewarding road to robbery?

In 1322 Robin got a new landlord, Thomas, Earl of Lancaster. When the Earl led a revolt against the weak and ill-advised King Edward II, Robin, like his fellow tenants, had no choice but to obey his lord's call to arms. But the revolt was crushed, and Lancaster was captured and

**Left:** *Robin Hood and Little John illustrating the 'Roxburghe Ballads' of around 1600.*

**Below:** *Romanticized view of a rustic couple, possibly Robin Hood and Maid Marian.*

beheaded for treason. His estates were confiscated by the King and the Earl's rebellious servants were outlawed.

Robin found a haven in Barnsdale Forest, an ideal hiding place covering 30 square miles of Yorkshire. And here we have the beginnings of the famous Sherwood Forest link.

---

Robin became an outlaw after a failed uprising against the unpopular King by his lord, the Earl of Lancaster

---

Sherwood was a neighbouring Nottinghamshire area of around 25 square miles. The two forests were served by the Roman-built Great North Road, used frequently by travellers who were obvious targets for outlaw robbers. The legend of Robin Hood, dressed in Lincoln green for camouflage in the forest, was born.

### THE LEGEND GROWS

Stories of Robin's death-defying, heroic antics became rife. There was the escapade involving the stuffy Bishop of Hereford, who was making his way to York when he came upon Robin and his men roasting venison poached from the King's hunting forests.

Thinking they were simple peasants the bishop ordered them to be seized immediately. The outlaws were unruffled, saying they were too busy to be arrested

and that food was uppermost in their minds. The bishop's aides then rounded them up, ignoring their pleas for mercy. But with one blast on Robin's horn the rest of the gang emerged from the forest, the bishop was taken prisoner and a ransom demanded.

Determined to get as much fun as possible from his hapless hostage, Robin made the bishop dance a jig around a large oak tree. To this very day, that spot is known as Bishop's Tree Root.

---

When the Bishop of Hereford tried to arrest Robin and his men they told him they were too busy eating stolen venison

---

We hear, too, of the day Robin, accompanied by his closest friend Little John, paid a visit to Whitby Abbey. The abbot asked them to display their much-heralded archery skills by shooting from the monastery roof. Robin and Little John were happy to oblige.

One of the best-loved stories about Robin, passed down from peasant to peasant, concerned his meeting with Edward II. Legend has it that the King, dismayed at his royal deer disappearing from under his eyes into the stomachs of the outlaws, made up his mind once and for all to clean up the forest.

He and his knights dressed up as monks and rode into Sherwood, knowing that Robin Hood and his band would be

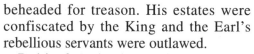

*Above left:King John in a legendary confrontation with the Abbott of Canterbury. Ever since Sir Walter Scott published* Ivanhoe *in 1819, storytellers have thought of Robin Hood as contemporary with John and his elder brother Richard Coeur-de-Lion.*

**Above:** *The men in Lincoln green take it easy with an armoured knight.*

**Above:** *Robin Hood depicted in combat with a foe. Their weapons are quarter staffs.*

**Right:** *Robin Hood and his band of outlaws face the wrath of King Richard in this undated version of the Sherwood myth.*

waiting for unfortunate travellers such as them. They were right. The outlaws intercepted them and demanded money.

The disguised king said that £40 was all he had (a small fortune in those days, anyway). Robin took £20 for his men and handed the rest back to the King.

Edward then produced a royal seal and told the outlaw leader that he was summoned to Nottingham to meet the King. Robin and his men dropped to their knees, swore love and allegiance to Edward and invited the 'monks' to dine with them - on the King's own venison!

Edward finally realized that Robin's unwittingly cheeky antics had thwarted him in his mission. He revealed his true identity and pardoned them, on condition that they all serve him at court if ever he called for them. This story sounds pure fantasy, dreamed up by admirers of Robin Hood over the centuries. But it may not be entire fiction, after all.

It is revealed in *A Lytell Geste of Robyn Hood*, published in 1459, and we know for a fact that the King was in Nottingham in 1332. We know too that the name Robin Hood appears in Edward's court accounts a few months later in 1324.

After that it seems he did one of his famous disappearing tricks, back into the forest and back once more into folklore.

---

**The secret network of routes in the forest was marked by trees known only to Robin and his followers**

---

And so the daring tales continue. There was Robin's visit to St Mary's church in Nottingham, where a monk recognized the outlaw and alerted the sheriff. Robin single-handedly slew twelve soldiers with his trusty sword before being captured. He must have known even then that his loyal followers would not abandon him. Before Robin could be brought to trial Little John led a fearless raid, repatriating Robin his leader to his outlaw 'family'. Just for good measure, they tracked down the monk who had 'grassed' on Robin - and murdered him.

THE COMPANIONS OF THE GREENWOOD

We cannot talk about Robin Hood without giving due credit to his Merry Men and to his legendary female companion Maid Marian. Robin's closest aide was Little John, supposedly not a merry man at all but a rather miserable, touchy fellow. It has always been believed that Little John was so called as a jest, and that he was in fact tall of stature. This was proved when his grave was opened at Hathersage, Derbyshire in 1784, and was found to contain the bones of an exceptionally tall man.

Friar Tuck is now believed to be a composite character of two fat friars, or perhaps even a single, jolly fellow who enjoyed morris dancing. He may even have been Robert Stafford, an early

fifteenth century Sussex chaplain who used the alias Friar Tuck to carry out his part-time business of outlaw.

As for Maid Marian, the latest research shows she was the product of a thirteenth-century French poem and, sadly, never kissed her sweetheart in the leafy glades of Sherwood Forest.

Her existence could also fit in with the theory that Robin was in fact 'born' out of a character depicted in May Day ceremonies. Maid Marian may simply have been Queen of the May.

WILL THE REAL ROBIN HOOD PLEASE STAND UP?

Robin Hood's legendary, leafy exploits in England's most famous forest continued until around 1346. He is reputed to have died, ill, at Kirklees Priory - his death hastened when the prioress, his cousin Elizabeth de Stainton, bled him until he

**Above:** *This engraving, entitled 'Courtesy of Little John', shows the outlaw apparently abasing himself before a knight - or possibly waylaying him in order to rob him.*

was too weak to recover from his crippling pains.

That's the romantic view of Robin Hood, valiant do-gooder. But there seems to be a strange Anglo-Saxon propensity to debunk their heroes, and Robin is one who has suffered more than most.

One expert, Graham Black, director of Nottingham's *The Tales Of Robin Hood* exhibition, said: 'We are now close to knowing Robin's true identity.'

According to Black, the real trail of Robin Hood starts in 1261 when William, son of Robert the Smith, was declared an outlaw in Berkshire. The court clerk who wrote the order gave him the nickname William Robehood or Robinhood.

Other court documents have been found which refer to people with the name Robinhood, and most of them were criminals. This suggests, say the scholars, that if the original Robin Hood existed he must have been active before that time.

The strongest candidate for this dubious honour, according to Graham Black, is Robert Hod, tenant of the Archbishopric of York, who fled from justice in 1225. He appears in records two years later as outlawed Hobbehod.

So where does the more romanticized version of the legend come from? Robin is generally thought of as being a contemporary of King Richard I, known as the Lionheart, who ruled from 1189 to 1199. But he was only placed there by Sir Walter Scott in his 1819 novel *Ivanhoe*.

In some versions of the tale Robin was a nobleman, the Earl of Huntingdon. But this again was an invention - of a playwright who in 1597 wanted to attract the nobility of the day to his theatre. Until that time Robin had been described as a yeoman, a retainer to a lord.

The elevation of Robin as the greatest archer in the land comes from wandering storytellers, who relayed to the simple people of rural England five ballads written between 1450 and 1500.

---

Maid Marian's virginal reputation was acquired only in the nineteenth century when the Victorians decided her act needed cleaning up

---

As for pure, chaste, virginal Maid Marian, she is supposedly the beautiful ward of evil Prince John, and first met Robin when she was ambushed by his Merry Men. But this theory is disregarded by academics, who say she first emerged in a thirteenth-century French poem as a shepherdess with her shepherd Robin.

It was not until two hundred years after the French poem was written that she was finally adapted to fit the Robin Hood legend. And Maid Marian's virginal reputation followed long after when the prudish Victorians cleaned up her act!

As for Friar Tuck, according to legend he was a jolly figure who ate huge meals, amused the outlaws with his jolly japes and fought doughtily with a staff. Indeed there was a real-life Friar Tuck. But he

**Below:** *This ancient drawing appears to show a soldier helping the collection of taxes from a penurious peasantry.*

was, in fact, a murderer and robber who was the chaplain of Lindfield parish in Sussex. He took the alias of Friar Tuck when a royal warrant demanded his arrest in 1417.

James Holt, professor of medieval history at Cambridge University and author of a book on Robin Hood, says: 'Records show that Friar Tuck organized a separate outlaw band 200 miles away from Sherwood Forest and hundreds of years after Robin Hood was active. And really, there was nothing jolly about Friar Tuck - he is believed to have burned and pillaged the homes of his enemies.'

Meanwhile Little John, generally regarded as a gentle giant who was Robin's right-hand man, was actually capable of brutal murder. John once slew a monk suspected of betraying Robin - then cut off the head of the monk's young servant so there would be no witness. He did perform one valiant act, however, when he rescued his master from the mightily fortified prison presided over by the notorious sheriff of Nottingham.

---

The jolly Friar Tuck was really a murderer and robber with a warrant out for his arrest

---

As for Robin, Professor Holt says: 'He was nothing like he is portrayed. He wore a hood, like a monk's cowl. There is absolutely no evidence that he robbed

from the rich to give to the poor. That was added to the legend two hundred years or more after his death. He was widely regarded as being a riotous marauder.'

Lovers of folklore much prefer Robin Hood's reputation to be that of fighting for the underdog, taking from those with money to give to those who had none, and all the while thumbing his nose at authority. Which is why it is nice to believe that, after a lifetime of daring deeds, whether for good or ill, our hero really did summon up enough strength as he lay dying to blow his horn and bring his faithful friend Little John to his side.

**Above:** *Robin Hood in the title page of an old volume. The Victorians maintained a highly romanticized version of the legend of the 'noble savage'.*

**Left:** *Could this be Robin and Maid Marian beneath a mighty forest oak? Only if tailors and hairdressers were in his merry band.*

# DINGO BABY
# Outback Injustice

'A dingo has got my baby!' cried distraught Australian mother Lindy Chamberlain. But her story was not believed. Were the family victims of prejudice and a cover-up by the authorities?

The news made just a few paragraphs in the world's press. And although it was a somewhat hollow victory, it was the closing chapter of a nightmare story for a young Australian mother.

Famous 'Dingo Baby Case' mum Lindy Chamberlain was awarded £210,000 damages for wrongful imprisonment. The compensation was reported in July 1991. It ended eleven years of fighting to see justice done.

But it was much less than Lindy felt she deserved. Three years of her life had been lost while she languished in jail for a crime she did not commit.

All the time, Lindy protested her innocence, telling anyone who would listen that it was a dingo, a wild dog, in the Australian desert that had taken and slaughtered her nine-week-old daughter. Followers of the case were shocked.

So too was Lindy. She couldn't understand how fellow human beings who had read her story and sat in judgement of her in court had decided she had committed such a wicked deed.

No one had believed that her screams were those of a mother at seeing her new baby dragged off by a wild animal. Yet the words Lindy Chamberlain cried that moment were to go down in history: 'A dingo has got my baby...!'

### 'DINGOES ARE WILD'

It was a scorching hot evening on 17 August 1980 when what had begun as a happy family camping holiday turned into tragedy. Lindy, her Seventh Day Adventist preacher husband Michael, and their three children Aidan, Reagan and baby Azaria were on a picnic near the mysterious Ayers Rock.

The Chamberlains had only casually glanced at a sign saying 'Dingoes are wild' and warning visitors not to encourage them by putting down food. Michael Chamberlain remained around the barbecue area when Lindy decided to return to the family tent to check on baby Azaria. The child had been left contentedly in her cot.

When Lindy entered the tent the scene before her eyes was too horrific to take in at first. She saw a dingo shaking her child violently in its clenched, bloody teeth. Then it ran off dragging the baby with it.

Fellow campers, visitors and other volunteers - three hundred in all - took part in a desperate search of the area. But no evidence of the poor child could be found on or around Ayers Rock, the sinister monolith sacred to the Aborigines.

Although there was no body, Alice Springs coroner Des Sturgess found at the inquest that 'in the time they went to the campsite and the time Mr Chamberlain was at the barbecue area, the death was caused'. Lindy could not be comforted. Her newborn baby had gone, dragged to a wild creature's lair somewhere and eaten.

---

When Lindy entered the tent she saw a dingo dangling her new baby Azaria from its bloodstained muzzle

---

That first inquest was gruelling enough for the Chamberlains, but the support of friends from Michael's Church and their families was a great help. What was to follow, however, was not only to invade their private grief but to lay it bare before an accusing world.

A year later they had to relive their baby's disappearance all over again. For some reason, Australia's Northern Territory police had not been satisfied with the inquest verdict. They worked towards disproving it and had, over the months, been gathering new evidence against Lindy Chamberlain. That

**Opposite:** *Lindy Chamberlain arrives at court in Darwin, Australia, for the inquiry into the death of her baby daughter Azaria - the so-called Dingo Baby.*

evidence was considered important enough to be presented before a second inquest in 1981.

The Chamberlains found themselves at the coroner's court again. This time a plastic bag lay on the table. It contained little Azaria's playsuit which had been found in shreds and blood-drenched outside a dingo's lair close to the campsite several days after the baby disappeared. What hadn't been found was the white matinee jacket Lindy said her child had been wearing.

The police forensic department had discovered a handprint the size of a woman's on the tiny garment. The team had come to the conclusion that the child's clothes had been touched with hands wet with blood. This could easily have been explained by the fact that Lindy, hysterical at what had happened, had clutched the baby's suit after accidentally smearing her hand in the blood that spattered the tent.

But more evidence was being compiled against her. They said they found blood on the door handle of the Chamberlains' car, on the carpet, under hinges and under the dashboard. Some traces were fetal blood, they said - the blood of a newborn baby.

### ACCUSED OF MURDER

The authorities now felt they had enough proof that a murder had taken place. They alleged that thirty-three-year-old Lindy Chamberlain had invented the dingo snatch story in a bid to get away with cold-bloodedly killing her baby.

---

**Without body or motive, and with only circumstantial evidence, the police decided Lindy had killed her own baby**

---

The investigations crossed the world. British forensic expert Professor James Cameron, of the London Hospital medical school, was called in to give a second opinion. It was claimed that Lindy had slashed her baby's throat with a pair of scissors as she sat in the family car. The bloodied child had then been held by human hands.

It is rare that a murder charge can be brought without a body being found. In this case there was no body, no motive and no weapon. But on 2 February 1982 the Alice Springs coroner, this time Gerry Galvin, made an announcement that stunned the Chamberlains. He ordered that Lindy should stand trial for murder. Michael was indicted as an accessory.

Even before that hearing, public feeling towards Lindy changed. She was no longer a mother who had lost her child in tragic, freak circumstances and therefore deserving of support and sympathy. She was now the cold and calculated killer of her very own baby.

By the time Lindy and her husband went to court on 19 April 1982 her cause had fiercely divided the nation. The case was discussed everywhere. Newspapers reported that Ayers Rock, sacred site for the Aborigines, was used for initiation and childbirth rites.

And it was revealed that the Chamberlains had visited other Aboriginal sites in the same area. Newspapers couldn't believe their luck when they heard that one of these sites was called Cut Throat Cave and that Azaria was the Aboriginal word for 'sacrifice in the wilderness'.

---

**The name Azaria, according to the journalists, meant 'sacrifice in the wilderness'**

---

It was obvious that Lindy and Michael Chamberlain, granted bail of £13,000 each, had the odds stacked against them for a fair hearing in Alice Springs. The authorities decided they should go to court in Darwin in a bid to get them impartial justice.

Their trial lasted seven weeks. The jury consisted of nine men and three women. They listened as the Chamberlains were first damned with the forensic evidence and then exonerated as loving parents, the victims of a tragic circumstance.

Prosecutor Ian Marker said Lindy killed her baby, buried her in the desert and then, with the help of her husband, dug the body up to tear off the clothing. They then placed the suit near a dingo's lair. He called Lindy's dingo claims a 'fanciful lie'.

Professor James Cameron did not waver from his conclusions. He stood by his original statement that, judging by Azaria's babysuit, death had been caused by an incised wound to her neck. In other words, by a cut throat.

*Below: Lindy and Michael Chamberlain's devout Seventh Day Adventist faith helped them through the nightmare ordeal that shattered their lives.*

Prosecuting evidence came from campsite witnesses, forensic scientists, police and lawyers. The defence called twenty-eight people to the stand. Among these were ten who said that Lindy was very loving towards Azaria.

Another two witnesses gave evidence that, the day before the baby went missing, two children at the campsite were confronted by a dingo that, obviously used to humans that put out food for it, showed no fear. It grabbed the trousers of one of the children.

The case seemed to be going well for the Chamberlains when a young man called Kyth Lenehan took the oath and told in a matter-of-fact way how he had been in an accident in June 1979, and that the caring Chamberlains had taken him to hospital in their car. He had bled quite heavily from a head injury. That would explain traces of blood found in their car.

Much later, forensic scientists were to be greatly embarrassed when the 'fetal blood' found under the car's dashboard turned out to be a bitumen substance used to dampen engine noise. And the holes in the baby's clothing were consistent with marks made by dingo teeth.

Mr Justice James Muirhead's summing up took a staggering six hours. Then the jury was out for several hours more.

Lindy and Michael showed no emotion when they were both found guilty.

## In prison Lindy gave birth to another daughter - taken from her only forty-five minutes later

Michael was found guilty of being an accessory and given an eighteenth-month suspended sentence. He was also bound over in the sum of £300 to be of good behaviour for three years.

The harsh sentence on Lindy shocked even those who had already believed her guilty - not just because she was still a young woman and the mother of two small children, but because when sentence was passed, on 29 October 1982, Lindy was just a month away from having another baby.

She gave birth to daughter Kahlia in prison. Forty-five minutes afterwards, her baby was taken away from her. Two days

later, Lindy was freed on bail pending an appeal. Lindy's appeal was rejected on 30 April 1983.

She was taken back to Berrinah jail in Darwin to 'resume her sentence as soon as possible'.

## NEW EVIDENCE OVERTURNS THE VERDICT

Then came a dramatic twist. In February 1986, climbers searching for the body of British tourist David Brett, who had fallen to his death on Ayers Rock, found a tiny bloodstained matinee jacket. It was the jacket of Azaria Chamberlain.

The police forensic scientists who had tried so hard to convict Lindy were now called in to examine what was delicately referred to as 'organic material' found near the jacket. It was human remains.

Lindy was let out of jail. One of her first actions was to instruct legal advisers to institute yet another inquiry.

The Royal Commission Inquiry began in May 1986 and lasted nearly a year. Heading it was Mr Justice Morling, who found many faults with the case presented by the prosecution. The Chamberlains were granted a pardon.

After all she had endured, this was not enough for Lindy. She said: 'There is no satisfaction in getting a pardon for something you didn't do... I want the conviction quashed and the authorities to admit I was wrongly accused.'

---

'There is no satisfaction getting a pardon for something you didn't do in the first place,' declared Lindy

---

Lindy and Michael were reunited while the legal system geared itself up for yet another hearing. Lindy talked of her time in jail. She said: 'I used to think I'd be out in a few days - that it was all a big mistake. The major thing that has got me through is my faith in God.'

On 15 September 1988, it took just ten minutes before three judges declared Lindy and Michael completely innocent of all charges.

As the verdict was announced, Lindy stared intently ahead. But as the court rose she almost fell back in her seat. Then she and Michael met the cheering crowd outside the Darwin court before going into hiding to pray.

The couple's lawyer announced he would institute proceedings to win compensation for all the time they had lived under sentence of killing their own baby. And he pointed out the true meaning of the baby's name, Azaria, which he said was 'Blessed of God'.

Lindy and her husband had fought for and won justice. But they were not yet able to retreat into a quiet life, biding their time until financial compensation was awarded.

## TELLING THE STORY

Thousands of miles away in London, film producer Verity Lambert had followed the Chamberlain story closely. She had read *Evil Angels* by Melbourne lawyer John Bryson, one of the nine books to be written about the infamous Dingo Baby Case. 'I felt very strongly there had been a miscarriage of justice and wanted to put the record straight,' she said.

Having set her heart on the story, Verity went to Australia to meet the Chamberlains. The film she eventually made was a £10 million production called *Cry in the Dark*.

---

Ignorant prejudice against Seventh Day Adventists had cooked up tales of ritual human sacrifice

---

The film won honours for its star, Meryl Streep, who was given the best actress award at the 1989 Cannes Film Festival. To prepare for the role, Meryl arranged a meeting with Lindy Chamberlain and said afterwards: 'The moment I read the story I knew I wanted to do the film. There was no question in my mind when I met her that she was innocent and I was very moved.'

Lindy also wrote her own version of events, in a 768-page book called *Through My Eyes*.

In 1991 the first reports of Lindy and Michael's cash settlements started to come through. In June that year the Northern Territory government agreed they could have £195,000. The couple

had asked for £690,000. The government had originally refused to pay anything, saying the Chamberlains had failed to declare all their assets accumulated from the sale of their story.

Lindy accused the authorities of deliberately delaying payments. She said: 'They know they have done me a wrong and have wronged the rest of my family, and that I'm innocent.'

Before the compensation award Michael Chamberlain had to cut firewood for a living and the children had no shoes

The Chamberlains desperately denied reports that they had made fortunes out of their story. Said Lindy: 'People laugh at you and some say "We know you've got money" but we just don't have any.'

The couple were heavily in debt to the Seventh Day Adventist Church. Michael was cutting up firewood for £15 a bundle, a job he was doing right up until the compensation award.

They did have a car, however - the 1970s vehicle in which Lindy was accused of murdering her baby. It was returned by the police authorities - minus its gearbox and engine.

Today the family still live in their bungalow in Cooranbong. Lindy maintains that her story of what really happened that night in 1980 was discredited by the authorities to protect its fledgling tourist industry and plans to develop facilities at Ayers Rock.

Lindy just wants an end to it all, but she says: 'You know, it never really did come out in evidence about a number of attacks on children before Azaria's death. The site where we camped is now part of an Aboriginal reserve. But I am told dingoes still come into tents...'

**Above:** *Even after Lindy Chamberlain was cleared of the murder of her baby, she had to convince a still - suspicious public that she had not made a fortune from her tragedy.*

# NESSIE
# Myth or Monster?

For many centuries Scottish folklore has told of a monster living in the murky depths of Loch Ness. Even modern hi-tech investigations have failed to prove whether Nessie and similar creatures from North America are fact or fiction

The existence of Nessie, the friendly monster of Loch Ness, was officially announced in 1933. But for countless generations dating back to the Dark Ages folklore had recounted the legend of the loch.

Deep, dark and forbidding, Loch Ness is a giant tear in the earth's surface cutting across the centre of Scotland. It is in an area as impenetrable and hostile as is possible in this modern age.

The Loch, 300 metres deep, 24 miles long, with water as black as pitch, was gouged out ten thousand years ago by the last of the Ice Age glaciers. And since man learned to pass on stories it has been home for mysterious monsters.

### THE LEGENDS BEGIN

The first written record of a water monster in the loch came as long ago as AD 565. In his biography of St Columba the then Abbot of Iona described how the saint triumphed over a 'water beast' in the River Ness. St Columba had been working to convert the heathen Picts and Scots from his new monastery on Iona, off the west coast of Scotland.

On his travels he came to Loch Ness and found local people burying a neighbour who had been badly mauled by Niseag - to give the monster her Gaelic name - while out swimming.

The corpse had been brought to the shore by villagers armed with grappling hooks to ward off the monster. But one of the saint's followers was foolhardy enough to swim across the narrows at the head of the Loch to get a small boat. As he swam out, 'a strange beast rose from the water something like a frog, only it was not a frog'.

---

St Columba is said to have ordered the great beast to turn back - and succeeded

---

St Columba, wrote the Abbot, faced the monster and ordered him: 'Go no further, nor touch that man.' Meekly, the monster turned on his tail and fled.

It was the beginning of the legend of the Loch Ness monster.

For centuries Scottish folklore has recounted tales of kelpies, malignant

**Above:** *Was this the Loch Ness monster - four dark humps in the water - photographed in 1952?*

**Opposite:** *In 1934, London gynaecologist Robert Wilson took four photographs of a strange creature rising from the depths of Loch Ness.*

water sprites, which lurked by the waterside disguised as horses, waiting for human victims.

Local people living near Loch Ness even now can remember being told as children not to swim in Loch Ness because of the kelpie.

## DETAILED SIGHTING

But it was in the spring of 1933 that Nessie was 'born' with the first famous detailed sighting, by Mr and Mrs John MacKay, which was reported in the *Inverness Courier*. In the same year a road had been blasted along the north shore and trees and undergrowth cut down to give a better view of the massive expanse of water, the largest freshwater lake in Britain.

In an interview in the *Daily Mail* fifty years later Mrs MacKay relived that dramatic day. She said:

*I was the only one who saw it. It was March 1933 and we were hurrying back from a house sale in Inverness. Suddenly at the seven-mile stone... you couldn't believe what we were seeing, never having seen such an enormous thing.*

*It was just an enormous black body, going up and down. You could not put a name to it. It could have been an*

**Top:** *Headquarters of the Loch Ness monster investigation team set up in 1968. Later expeditions were to use ever more sophisticated equipment.*

**Above:** *Members of the team of monster hunters watch the loch's surface, eager for any sign of the creature's existence.*

*elephant or a whale. I was yelling to John to stop, stop - whatever words came into my head - but he only thought that a bee was bothering me on my wind-screen, you had to remember it was the old road, very narrow and by the time he stopped...*

'Just ripples...' said her husband. He swore her to secrecy, explaining: 'If that got round they'd all be saying we've been imbibing. Put more water in it, they'd say.'

But Mrs MacKay did tell her story. She said 'I told someone in the strictest confidence, who then told someone else and the water bailiff Alex Campbell got to hear of it. He was local correspondent for the *Courier*.'

---

If they told their amazing story, Mr MacKay thought, people would shake their heads in disbelief and say the couple had been drinking

---

The editor printed the story under the headline 'Strange Spectacle of Loch Ness', and for the first time described it as a monster. It caused a sensation - and an explosion of sightings.

## THE SIGHTINGS MUSHROOM

In the next fifty years there were over three thousand serious claims that Nessie was alive and well. Could they all be mistaken?

Just two months after the MacKay sighting a gang of workmen engaged on blasting operations were startled to see Nessie going up the centre of the lake in the wake of a passing drifter. They said that it had an 'enormous head' and a large, heavy body.

And in August of the same year three witnesses noticed a disturbance on the surface of a very calm Loch Ness. There were several humps in line, rising and falling with a slightly undulating motion suggesting a caterpillar.

Sightings came thick and fast. In 1938 a steam tug captain and his mate were astonished to notice a huge, black 'animal' shaped rather like a hump-backed whale emerge on the surface and keep up with their vessel.

The creature had two distinct humps, but after a brief disappearance it resurfaced with seven humps or coils and sped past the tug 'at terrific speed' leaving large waves.

On 13 August 1960, the Rev W.L. Dobb had just finished a picnic lunch with his family beside the lake when they all saw large waves moving along the water. A few seconds later they all saw a large black hump. It quickly disappeared - to be replaced by two humps.

It is as though Nessie is playing a tantalizing game of hide-and-seek with sightseers and scientists.

## PHOTOGRAPHIC EVIDENCE

But beside eye-witness reports there is photographic evidence to support the existence of the mysterious monster.

Photographers began arriving to picture Nessie within months of the MacKay spotting. In November 1933 the Rev N. Dundas, who saw Nessie with his wife, tried to photograph the beast - but when the photo was developed the monster was missing.

The first photograph alleging to show Nessie was taken by Hugh Gray, also in 1933. Gray took five pictures - but four were blank. When his photograph was published in various newspapers Kodak staff signed a statement that the negative had not been tampered with.

In 1934 came the famous 'Surgeon's Photograph'. Robert Wilson was a London gynaecologist on holiday with a friend. They were driving to Inverness and had stopped on the road by the Loch.

Suddenly he noticed a commotion in the water 'between 150 and 200 yards from the shore where the head of some strange animal rose up out of the water'. He managed to take four photographs before the object sank from view.

**Below:** *Even submarines have been used in the hunt for Nessie. Some detected strange, moving objects in the loch's depths.*

**Above:** *Fiction not fact... A film-maker touches up the paintwork of a plastic Nessie on the lochside, for the spoof movie,* **The Private Life of Sherlock Holmes.**

The third important photograph supporting the theory that Nessie does exist was taken by Lachlan Stuart in July 1951. He was employed by the Forestry Commission and lived close to the Loch with his wife and children and a lodger, Taylor Hay.

---

Given the huge quantity of detailed evidence from eye-witnesses, can they all have been mistaken?

---

But sceptics say that photographs of Nessie are either faked or misinterpreted. Logs in the water, the wake of passing vessels or wind changes could cause images similar to Nessie, they argue. But the sheer volume and intensity of eye-witness evidence from Loch Ness cannot be ignored. Is it possible that they are all liars or just plain mistaken?

Some eye-witnesses believe that Nessie can live on land as well as water. As a child during World War I Margaret Cameron heard 'crackling' in the trees and saw a creature slither down into the water. She said, 'It had a huge body and its movement was like a caterpillar.'

It had a shiny skin, the colour of an elephant, and two short round feet at the front. After lurching to one side it put one foot after the other into the water.

Mr and Mrs George Spicer from London described it in 1933 as a 'loathsome sight'. It looked like a huge snail with a long neck, he said. And it was carrying what looked like a dead lamb in its mouth.

---

Sceptics say the 'Monster' is merely an otter, and that the peculiar light on the Loch plays tricks with people's eyes

---

Some experts have used these land-based sightings to argue that Nessie was nothing but an otter and witnesses were confused by tricks of the light.

The Loch itself does present problems because of its situation. It can play tricks on the eyes. It is a large mass of water, sometimes completely calm in a way that the sea rarely is, and its high shoreline casts deep shadows and reflections.

### HI-TECH COMES TO LOCH NESS

The locals in the area - ever ready to coin a shilling as only a Scotsman can - have been only too willing to boost their tourist industry with less than scientific evidence of the monster's existence.

Modern technology, however, has made the hunt for the truth about Nessie more scientific and reliable. Two cine films of the Loch, which are far more difficult to fake than still photographs, were submitted to the Joint Air Reconnaissance Intelligence Centre by David James of the Loch Ness Investigation Bureau.

The first was shot by Tim Dinsdale and shows a hump moving slowly away from him and then fast across his field of vision while submerging. The analysts concluded that the object was 'probably animate'. They said that the object was nearly 5 ft 6 in wide and moved at about 10 miles per hour.

In 1970 underwater photography was used as an investigative aid for the first time. But the murkiness of the peaty water and the limitations of equipment make it difficult.

This photographic expedition was led by Dr Robert Rines, president of the Academy of Applied Science in Belmont,

Massachusetts. Rines stayed two weeks, and two years later produced photos showing a fin or flipper.

His second visit, in 1975, resulted in a picture which could be interpreted as the upper torso, neck and head of a living creature. But other investigations into the circumstances of how the photograph was taken have tended to denigrate the veracity of the picture.

---

Is Nessie a plesiosaur, a relic from before the last Ice Age 70 million years ago?

---

However it was enough for naturalist Sir Peter Scott, who had helped launch the Loch Ness Phenomena Investigation Bureau in 1962. He announced: 'There are probably between twenty and fifty of them down there. I believe they are related to the plesiosaurs.'

The plesiosaur has not been seen on earth for 70 million years. Monster hunters concluded that Nessie and her ancestors were cut off from the sea when the Loch was formed at the end of the last Ice Age. But other experts argued that the plesiosaur could never have survived in the conditions of Loch Ness, or would never have coped in its original form and would need to have mutated drastically to live.

### NESSIE'S RELATIVES ABROAD

But while Nessie may be the most famous of her breed there are other water monsters haunting lakes and seas all over the world. She is not alone.

In Lake Okanagan in British Columbia, near the US-Canada border, reputedly lives a monster named the great Ogopogo. In fact verifiable sightings were being recorded a long time before Nessie's notoriety.

The first reports of the monster of the lake originated with the Indians in the seventeenth century. They described a large, dark-coloured creature with a long neck and a humped back.

The beast's name means 'remorseful one', for in Indian legend he was a murderer who had been changed into a water serpent in punishment.

**Below:** *The Japanese are obsessive Nessie hunters. Here she is represented, complete with spouting nostrils, in Dago Park, Fukuoka City, Kyushu.*

The modern spate of sightings started in the 1870s, when Susan Allison saw what she thought was a log suddenly swim up-lake against the wind. In July 1890 Captain Thomas Shorts was sailing the steamer *Jubilee* through the lake when he saw an animal off Squally Point, about 15 ft long, with a ram-like head and the sun shining through its fins.

Arthur Folden, a sawmill worker, was driving his wife home on a sunny day in August 1968 when they saw something large and animate moving through the calm water of the lake. Folden stopped the car and and took out his 8mm cine camera.

For a minute he filmed the object, which was swimming about 200 yards from the shore. Scared of the publicity, he waited a year before he was persuaded by relatives to show the film publicly.

---

In Indian legend the Ogopogo was a murderer who had been turned into a water monster to punish him

---

In 1976 there was more photographic evidence. Ed Fletcher was on the lake when an object cut across his bow. He recorded: 'If I hadn't shut the engine off I could have run him over or jumped on his back. The boat drifted to within 30 feet of him.'

Fletcher and his daughter, Diane, had time to return to shore to pick up a camera. When they returned, Ogopogo appeared from the depths again.

Fletcher, his daughter and another passenger whom they had picked up at the same time as the camera watched for an hour. 'He would submerge, swim at least two city blocks, then surface and all the while we chased him.'

He said that the serpent surfaced a dozen times. Fletcher took five photographs. He reported that it swam coiled up and then it stretched out.

His daughter described the skin as smooth and brownish like that of a whale, with small ridges on its back. As it swam it turned like a corkscrew. And the witnesses also talked of its head which, they said, had 'two things standing up from the head like the ears of a Dobermann pinscher'.

MORE WATER MONSTERS

A monster named Manipogo - presumably a relation of Ogie - is believed to inhabit the two lakes of Manitoba and Winnipegosis in Canada. Again, it was originally seen by Indians. Most descriptions give it a flat, snake-like head, dark skin and three humps. Some reports have even given it a mate and offspring.

---

Some reports say that the creature known as Manipogo has a mate and young

---

Lake Champlain, which straddles the Canadian-US border, is also famous for monster sightings. 'Champ' was first spotted by Samuel de Champlain, after whom the lake was named, in 1609. He thought it looked like a 20 ft snake with a horse's head.

An amazing picture allegedly of Lake Champlain's mystery creature was taken by Sandra Mansi in 1977. Some sceptics try to suggest that the head and neck are

really the fin of a small whale rolling on its side. Others contend there was a sand-bar just below the surface, implying that it was a hoax.

---

One set of experts said the photograph was genuine. Another said the creature was as real as the tooth fairy

---

The Optical Sciences Centre at the University of Arizona examined the print and said it was genuine. But Professor Paul Kurtz of the State University of New York said he thought that the monster was as real as the tooth fairy.

Ireland, too, has its lake monsters. Even three priests swore that they'd seen an unknown being in Lough Ree. On 18 May 1960 the three Fathers - Daniel Murray, Matthew Burke and Richard Quigly - were fishing off the Lough in the River Shannon.

Suddenly the peace was shattered by a large flat-headed creature approaching them. It was about 100 yards from where they sat. All three of the priests could see it quite clearly.

## THE MYSTERY GOES ON

But as sightings continue all over the world, even the great advances of science do not seem to be getting us any nearer proving - or disproving - the existence of Nessie and her colleagues.

In 1933 E.G. Boulenger, Director of the Aquarium at London Zoo, said that reports of Nessie were 'a striking example of mass hallucination'. He pointed out that once Nessie was seen by a few people, she would be reported by many more. People see what they want to see, he argued. But can so many thousands be deceived worldwide?

Scientists have argued that there is no fish, reptile, mammal or amphibian known to them which matches the descriptions of the monsters of the lakes.

We know that the giant monsters who lived on land died out because they could not adapt. But we do not know what happened to the species who were at home in the water.

Perhaps down there lazing in the dark depths of Loch Ness and other lakes around the world lies the answer.

**Above:** *A sea 'monster' spotted off the coast of California. Sightings of Nessie-like creatures have been reported from all over the globe - and are increasing.*

# GHOSTS
# Terrors of the Night

Why did an English schoolboy's furniture move spontaneously about his bedroom? What did a tough sailor see in an empty house that frightened him to death? Believe them or not, you have to agree that these stories of the supernatural are bizarre - and scary

**G**hosts, haunted houses and castles, things that go bump in the night, poltergeists - they are the stuff of our worst nightmares. Eerie, pale reminders of our own mortality and the uncertainty which awaits us all. Are they real...or merely the products of over-creative minds?

You be the judge as we investigate some of history's most famous hauntings...from the White House to the Bank of England to the tiny town of Amityville, Long Island, to Hollywood.

## THE WHITE HOUSE APPARITION

Winston Churchill has seen him, so has visiting Dutch Princess Juliana. And Maureen Reagan, the former President's first daughter, swears by him. Who is he?

**Above left:** *The apparition of assassinated American President Abraham Lincoln has been seen regularly in the White House over the years.*

**Above:** *Winston Churchill claimed to have seen the ghost of Abraham Lincoln.*

**Opposite:** *The ghost of Dorothy Walpole is said to haunt Raynham Hall in Norfolk. This photograph showing what seems to be a ghostly presence coming down the stairs was taken in 1936.*

**Left:** *Too much familiarity with the spiritual could be dangerous in 17th-century Salem, Massachusetts. This painting depicts the trial of George Jacobs, one of Salem's infamous witchcraft trials.*

Well, according to those who have caught a glimpse of the apparition, it's none other than Abraham Lincoln, America's greatest President.

'I'm not kidding,' says Maureen Reagan. 'We've really seen it.' She and her husband, Dennis Revell, often slept in Lincoln's Bedroom when they visited her parents in Washington, and claim to have seen the apparition, which is sometimes red, sometimes orange. Maureen and her husband claim it's Lincoln's ghost.

---

The Reagans' dog refused ever to set foot in the Lincoln Bedroom, where their daughter had seen an apparition

---

Neither President Reagan nor Nancy ever saw the apparition during their eight-year stay in the White House, and nor have President Bush or First Lady Barbara. Mrs Reagan scoffed at the notion that Lincoln's spirit still wandered the historic building, but she does recall that the family dog, Rex, often barked in the bedroom's direction - and refused ever to set foot in it.

### THE GHOSTS OF FLIGHT 401

Ghosts, however, aren't restricted to houses or castles. One of the most famous of all spooky tales is that of the Ghosts of Flight 401. In December 1972, an Eastern Airlines TriStar crashed into a murky Florida swamp, killing 101 people

**Above left:** *James Brolin played the part of George Lutz in the film version of* **The Amityville Horror.**

**Above:** *Police guard the house at Amityville, Long Island, that became the focus of the horror story industry.*

**Below:** *Margot Kidder and James Brolin portrayed the couple who bought their dream home, only to have it turn into a nightmare.*

including the pilot and his flight engineer. But since the accident Captain Bob Loft and engineer Dan Repo have been spotted on at least twenty other Eastern TriStar jetliners by crew members.

---

Startled TriStar crew members have claimed sightings of the pilot and engineer of the ill-fated Flight 401

---

Most of the sightings - by highly trained aviators who are hardly prone to panic - have occurred on planes that were fitted with parts of Flight 401 that were salvaged. And many of those who swear they have seen the ghosts of Loft and Repo knew both men personally.

## HOLLYWOOD'S BRUSH WITH THE SUPERNATURAL

More than 25 million Americans claim to have seen a ghost, so it comes as no surprise that many Hollywood stars have also had brushes with the supernatural. Actress Elke Sommer actually bought a haunted house in Beverly Hills - though she had no idea it was home to a ghost before she moved in.

But soon after she and Joe Hyams moved in, as they were lying in their bedroom, they began to hear weird noises coming from the dining room downstairs. Every night was the same, until a few weeks later when they were suddenly awakened by a loud knocking on their bedroom door. Hyams jumped out of bed, opened the door and saw nothing - nothing except a cloud of thick black smoke coming from downstairs.

Startled, he raced down the stairs, and found the dining room ablaze. No one knows what happened for certain, but several mediums told the couple that the ghost had probably started the fire as a prank, but then changed his mind and raced upstairs to warn them.

---

Did the ghost in Elke Sommer's Beverly Hills mansion start a fire as a prank, and then warn the inhabitants?

---

Oscar-winner Ellen Burstyn, who starred in *One Flew Over the Cuckoo's Nest*, has also had a run-in with a ghost - but not only was this ghost friendly, she knew him. She recalled that shortly after the death of Lee Strasberg, the famed acting tutor, in 1981 she was staying with his widow in the Strasbergs' apartment.

As she tried to fall asleep, his ghost appeared to her and spoke. 'I suddenly felt a pull on my shoulder, and Lee appeared,' she said. 'He said to me, "Be strong. Yes, grieve, but death is part of life, and not the end." '

Even more frightening, however, was the experience of James Brolin, star of *The Amityville Horror*, who claims the movie was surrounded by evil during its making. He recalled:

*On the very first day of filming I stepped in the elevator in my apartment block and pressed the button for the lobby floor. Before we'd gone three floors it shuddered to a grinding, screeching halt, the lights flickered and I was plunged into frightening darkness. I screamed for help, but no one could hear me. It was an eerie, frightening experience. You imagine all sorts of hair-raising things in silent darkness. It seemed an eternity.*

Thirty minutes later the elevator restarted, and a relieved Brolin went to the set of the film.

## GHOSTLY HORRORS

The macabre story chronicled in Brolin's film was, of course, far scarier than anything that ever happened to the actor. The story of *The Amityville Horror* still ranks as one of the most terrifying ever.

The tale began one November night in 1974 when Ronald DeFeo, then twenty-three, gruesomely slaughtered his family of six in their six-bedroom house in suburban Long Island. Thirteen months later, land surveyor George Lutz and his

**Below:** *Ronald DeFeo is led from Suffolk county police headquarters accused of gruesomely slaughtering his family of six.*

**Bottom:** *Just as the owner George Lutz claimed to have done, actor Brolin takes on the characteristics of murderer DeFeo who previously lived in the Amityville house.*

family moved into that very same house - and within twenty-eight days, they would flee for their lives.

The story of 112 Ocean Avenue, which Jay Anson developed into a best-selling book, stunned America. The Lutzes' eerie account included green slime oozing from the walls, large numbers of flies, doors coming loose off their hinges, the sounds of a band playing in the living room and pigs snorting in the windows. Finally, after they and their young children could take no more of the horrifying haunting, they fled, leaving behind virtually everything.

---

'I switched on my lamp,' recalled Matthew Manning, 'and saw to my horror that the cupboard was inching out from the wall towards me'

---

Englishman Matthew Manning had a similarly terrifying experience with unseen forces in Cambridge, beginning in 1967. When he was just eleven, the house he shared with his parents was suddenly overtaken by strange events. His father, Derek, noticed that every time he reset a silver mug on a shelf it would fall to the floor. Over the next few weeks other objects were found in places they shouldn't have been, and gradually the off-putting disturbances became more than frightening. Heavy objects, like chairs and tables, began moving about

**Left:** *Ronald DeFeo leaves court, convicted of murder. Thirteen months later, surveyor George Lutz and his wife bought the death house.*

**Below:** *No. 112 Ocean Avenue, Amityville, drove the Lutz couple away within twenty-eight days of their purchasing the six-bedroom house.*

The next day, he and his parents awoke to find the house a shambles: furniture was strewn about, pictures had fallen from the walls, a table had been turned upside down and there were ornaments scattered about the floor.

Eventually, the sinister events became even more frightening. Water pools appeared on the floor and, most eerily, writing began appearing on the wall. One message warned: 'Matthew Beware'.

Incredibly, however, when Matthew left for boarding school the poltergeist went with him, doing the same bizarre things to the dormitory as it had done to his parents' house. It wasn't until 1971 that Matthew began to develop psychic skills of his own, and gradually the poltergeist activity ceased.

Not all poltergeist appearances are so terrifying, however. The story of Francis Martin and his family would seem to bear that out. In October 1963, Mr Martin noticed a damp area appearing on the wall of the living room in his home in Methuen, Massachusetts.

Suddenly there was a loud popping sound and a gush of water burst from the wall, lasting for some twenty seconds. After a few days of sudden water spurts, the anxious family moved into a relative's house nearby.

---

The Martin family moved to a relative's house to escape the strange happenings - but their poltergeist came with them

---

and tipping over. Matthew, who recounted some of the frightening moments in his book *The Link* recalled:

*I had gone to bed...I suddenly heard a scraping noise coming from the direction of the cupboard, which continued for almost thirty seconds. Having listened to it for a moment, I switched on my lamp and saw to my horror that the cupboard was inching out from the wall towards me. When it halted, it had advanced about eighteen inches. I switched off the light and almost simultaneously my bed started to vibrate violently back and forth...[then] the vibrating ceased, and I felt the bottom end of my bed rising from the floor to what I estimated to be about one foot.*

**Above:** *Popular conception of a ghostly apparition. In a survey, more than 25 million Americans claimed to have seen a ghost.*

Whatever had caused their problem followed - and soon the second house was spurting water! A deputy fire inspector came around to investigate and checked the structure for leaky pipes, but found none. Not wanting to inundate the relative's house, the Martin family returned to their own home...but not before turning the water off at the main and draining the pipes.

It did no good, however, and the bizarre water flow from the walls continued unabated. The strange phenomenon occurred on and off over the next few weeks, but then stopped as suddenly as if someone - or something - had turned off a tap.

### HAUNTED LONDON

While America has its fair share of ghostly doings, London is probably home to more famous ghosts than any other city in the world. From out-of-the-way back streets to famed landmarks like the Tower, the Bank of England and Kensington Palace, the city is haunted with literally hundreds of spirits.

The Bank of England, for instance, has been haunted by the Black Nun, an apparition that wanders around the Bank garden. The ghost is said to be Sarah Whitehead, the sister of a former Bank employee, Philip Whitehead, who was arrested in 1811 for forging cheques. Whitehead was sentenced to death, and the tragedy so traumatized his sister that for the next twenty-five years she went daily to the Bank to look for him.

When she died, she was buried in an old church inside the Bank grounds, which later became the Bank gardens. In the 150 years or so since, she has been sighted on numerous occasions - still wandering in her eternal search for her long dead brother.

Probably the most famous and scariest of all the city's ghosts is the one which haunts a house in Berkeley Square - an apparition that reportedly scared at least three people to death. One of the stories surrounding the Berkeley Square ghost tells of a young child who was either tortured or frightened to death in the house's nursery. His ghost, still sobbing

**Above left:** *Matthew Manning was haunted by poltergeist activity from the age of eleven.*

**Above:** *Matthew Manning's poltergeists only left him alone when he began to develop psychic powers of his own.*

**Below**: *One of Manning's more remarkable psychic gifts was 'automatic' drawing. This is a rhinoceros drawn by him in the style of the Renaissance artist Albrecht Dürer.*

and wearing a kilt-like garment, is said to make periodic appearances.

Another story claims the ghost is actually that of a young woman, who shared the house with her lascivious uncle. In an attempt to free herself of his immoral advances, she threw herself from a window on the top floor. People claimed to have seen her ghost hanging on to the ledge and screaming.

---

Is the Bank of England's ghost the sister of an employee sentenced to death for forging cheques?

---

A third story recounts the bizarre tale of a white-faced man whose appearance was so ghastly, that a sailor was literally frightened to death by the apparition when he visited the house with a crew mate.

The building was vacant at the time, so the two seamen decided to sleep there - only to be awakened by the sound of footsteps coming up the stairs. Someone - or something - walked into their room, causing one of the poor chaps to panic so much that he fell from a window to his death. The second sailor, who survived the terrifying ordeal, was later found on the street, unconscious from fear.

The house was so famous in Victorian days that it actually became a tourist spot of sorts. One well-heeled citizen, Lord Lyttleton, actually spent a night inside the haunted room, armed with two rifles which he had loaded with buckshot and

unearthly visitor. The most famous, of course, is the Man in Grey, who has been spotted by dozens of startled actors and patrons in the past two hundred years.

He appears in knee breeches, frock coat and tricorn hat, and is most often seen walking along the gangway from one side of the theatre to the other - where he disappears through the wall. Occasionally the Man in Grey has been spotted in one of the seats. His ghostly appearance at the beginning of a show is said to forecast a successful run. Most of the cast of *The Dancing Years* claim they saw him when they gathered on stage for a photo shoot.

---

**The appearance of the Man in Grey at the Theatre Royal, Drury Lane is supposed to ensure a successful run**

---

According to theatre historians, about one hundred years ago, a small room was discovered inside the theatre, containing the skeleton of a man with a knife between his ribs. They believe he was the victim of a ruthless eighteenth-century manager of the theatre.

The theatre is also thought to be haunted by the ghost of Dan Leno, the comedian-dancer. In the dressing room he used during his tenure at the theatre - the number of which is kept a secret in case it upsets the current tenant - a face sometimes appears in the mirror. Those who have seen it swear it is Leno's.

There have been a number of peculiar happenings at the theatre which would tend to support those who claim to have seen at least one of the ghosts. Some actors swear they have been pushed or nudged by 'unseen hands' while on stage, and Michael Crawford said a hand assisted him during one difficult scene. Indeed, theatre archivist George Hoare has claimed the unseen hands tugged on his coat as he was leaving his office.

The Drury Lane Theatre may be the most famous of London's haunted theatres, but it's by no means the only one. In fact, five other theatres claim to have ghosts, including the spirit of John Buckstone, whose appearance is also said to guarantee a show's success.

Buckstone, who was actor-manager at

silver sixpences, which he believed would guarantee him protection against whatever evil lurked inside. He survived the night, but later recounted firing at an apparition that leaped at him from the dark. He also claimed he tracked down a woman who had been driven insane after spending a night inside the house.

---

**Armed with buckshot and silver bullets, Lord Lyttleton spent a night inside the notorious Berkeley Square house**

---

Throughout the long and macabre history of the house, two other people are said to have died from fright. One, a housemaid, was found inside the haunted room, hysterically weeping on the floor. She was taken to St George's Hospital, where she died the very next day.

But before her death, doctors tried to ascertain what had scared her so much. She refused to discuss it, saying only it was 'just too horrible' to describe. Not long after, a volunteer agreed to spend a night in the room to learn what may have happened. He was found later that night - his eyes agape in horror, and dead.

Whatever evil lies in wait inside the house in Berkeley Square, it has reportedly been dormant for many years.

The Theatre Royal in Drury Lane is another of London's famous haunted landmarks - but the three centuries-old building may have more than just one

*Top: **One message that appeared mysteriously on Manning's bedroom wall warned: 'Matthew Beware'.***

*Above: **'Slavery', a monkey - another of Matthew Manning's automatic drawings.***

The ghost who haunts the Coliseum is said to be a young soldier of World War I, who appears to take his seat in the dress circle on the anniversary of his death. It's said he spent his last night in London at the theatre, watching the pretty ladies of the show. The next day, he left for the battlefield and was killed.

## ROYAL APPARITIONS

From clowns to kings - London has them all. At Kensington Palace, numerous people over the years swear to have seen the face of King George II looking out of the window over the main entrance.

Nearing death, the King was said to stare longingly out of the window at the weathervane, in the hope that the winds would signal a good breeze for the ships bringing him despatches from his beloved Germany - despatches he dearly wanted to read before the end came. But on 25 October 1760 he died - with the winds still unfavourable to shipping.

His sad, ghostly face is said still to peer out occasionally at the vane, hoping for a change in the wind.

**Above:** *The Bank of England is said to be haunted by the ghost of 'the black nun'.*

**Below:** *The Tower of London housing the royal jewellery collection, scene of several hauntings.*

the Haymarket Theatre, was a favourite of Queen Victoria. His ghost, which is considered very friendly by those who have seen it, appears in one of the boxes, and his old dressing room door opens and closes by itself. The Haymarket is also haunted by the ghost of Henry Field, who was an actor-manager there during the eighteenth century.

Of course, no discussion of famous London hauntings would be complete without reference to the Tower - which has been home to numerous bizarre events over the centuries.

One of the eeriest reports of strange goings on comes from Edward Swifte, Keeper of the Crown Jewels for almost forty years until his retirement in 1852.

Swifte recalled that one night, in October 1817, he was dining with his family inside the sitting room of the Jewel House when they saw the most bizarre sight: 'A cylindrical figure, like a glass tube' hovering above their table for as long as two minutes. Suddenly, the 'tube' - which Swifte described as having been filled with a dense, blue-and-white liquid - began moving around the table. Mrs Swifte screamed: 'Oh, Christ! It has seized me!' At that, Swifte jumped to his feet and swung at the object with his chair. In the blink of an eye, the mysterious tube vanished.

Incredibly, neither Swifte's son nor sister-in-law had seen a thing!

---

**Field Marshal Lord Grenfell saw the ghost of Anne Boleyn - and was court martialed for being drunk**

---

One of the most astonishing apparitions inside the historic landmark is an actual execution. According to those who have witnessed the frightening spectacle, the execution is that of the Countess of Salisbury, who was beheaded by order of King Henry VIII.

The apparition appears only on the anniversary of her death, and eye-witnesses say she can be clearly seen and heard screaming in terror as she is chased by her ghostly executioner. The ghastly apparition ends with her decapitation.

Not surprisingly, the Bloody Tower is home to most of the Tower of London's ghostly sightings, including those surrounding the two little Princes, King Edward V and his younger brother, Richard, Duke of York. They were murdered on the orders of Richard, Duke of Gloucester, later King Richard III. Their tiny ghosts have been spotted many times, walking hand in hand, on their eternal quest for peace.

The headless body of Anne Boleyn, one of several executed wives of Henry VIII, has been seen in several places throughout the Tower of London.

Field Marshal Lord Grenfell, who was stationed at the Tower as a young lieutenant, swore that he saw Anne's ghost, outside the King's Houses, where she was kept on the evening before her execution. He said her headless body appeared in front of him, and then he fainted. His superiors didn't believe him, claiming he was drunk, but at the subsequent court martial, when other guards told similar tales, he was acquitted.

*Below: Churches too have their fair share of hauntings. This picture which seems to show the ghostly figure of a priest was taken at Eastry, Kent, in 1956.*

# SPACE INVADERS
## UFOs and Aliens

Is there intelligent life elsewhere in the universe? And if so, are UFOs - Unidentified Flying Objects - a sign of its existence? Sceptics may mock, but the weight of evidence is mounting and governments take the matter very seriously indeed

**Left:** *Former US President Jimmy Carter is a firm believer in UFOs - he claims to have seen one.*

**Opposite:** *Four supposed UFOs appear as glowing blobs above a car park and factory in 1950s America.*

**Below:** *This photograph, allegedly showing five UFOs flying in formation, appeared in a weekly Dublin newspaper for teenagers.*

The first encounters hardly compared with Steven Spielberg's vision. There was no meeting of minds, no mother ship; there were no bug-eyed humanoids - not even a lyrical conversation between computers.

Instead, the first telltale meeting, which came on 24 June 1947, was nothing but a fleeting glimpse on the horizon. Idaho businessman Kenneth Arnold, who was piloting his own small plane, was flying over Washington State when he saw nine 'saucer-like things' which were flying in formation, at speeds he would later estimate at some 1200 miles an hour.

His sensational report, which gave birth to the term 'flying saucer', began the twentieth-century fixation with Unidentified Flying Objects, which in less than fifty years has resulted in thousands of sightings.

Everyone, from policemen via pilots and astronomers to former President Jimmy Carter, claims to have seen the mysterious objects - while others swear they have actually made contact with the 'extraterrestrial' visitors. President Carter, who sighted a UFO on the night of 6 January 1969, while he was still Governor of Georgia, has said: 'I'm convinced that UFOs exist, because I have seen one.'

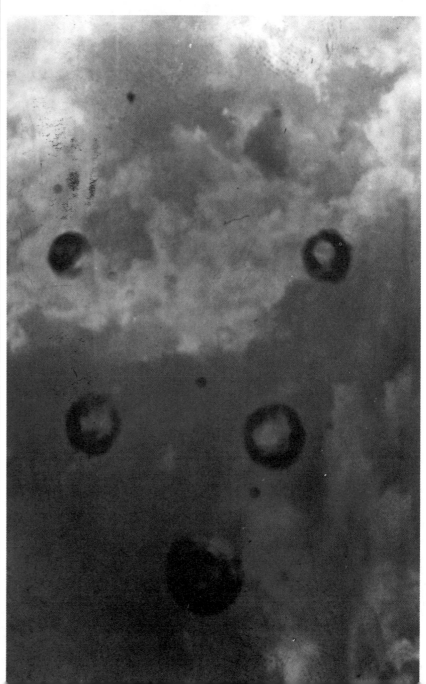

## ARE WE ALONE?

But before any serious discussion on the existence or otherwise of UFOs can be undertaken, our first question must be: are we alone?

The answer, of course, has never been conclusively proven...and yet even the most learned of scientists calculate the odds heavily in favour of us not having the universe entirely to ourselves. Planet earth and our entire solar system are part of one average-size galaxy called the Milky Way, which contains 200 billion stars similar to our own sun. Since most of these stars are believed to have satellites or 'planets' of their own, even the most cautious scientist will admit that millions of planets in our galaxy may be capable of supporting some type of life form in some stage of evolution.

*Above: The charred remains of a supposed alien, found in Mexico by Charles Wilhelm and his wife Geri.*

*Right: UFO sightings have been reported throughout the world - and sometimes people have provided photographic 'evidence'. This picture was taken in Denmark.*

So given that intelligent life almost certainly exists elsewhere in the universe, the argument for the existence of UFOs becomes even more plausible.

But that is not to say all such sightings are real. In fact, even firm believers in UFOs admit that some 95 per cent of all 'sightings' are easily explainable in earthly terms - that is, they are the result of natural phenomena or natural objects misidentified. According to scientific studies, the most common sources of UFO misidentifications are meteors, stars and planets, airplanes, weather balloons, clouds, satellites and simple mirages.

---

The Milky Way, of which our solar system is merely a part, contains 200 billion stars similar to our sun

---

But what of the remaining 5 per cent - which even the most ardent debunker cannot fully explain away? Where do they come from? And why?

No one knows whence they come, but some UFO proponents believe they know why. According to their scenario, the most common theory is that these extraterrestrial beings have been monitoring earth at intervals for hundreds of years. Indeed, advocates note that in 1270 the citizens of Bristol recorded seeing a strange flying craft over the city - and that one of its occupants was 'burned and asphyxiated' by the earth's atmosphere when it got out of the craft!

In 1561 the citizens of Nuremberg in Germany claimed they had seen several circular objects which 'appeared to fall to

the ground as if all was on fire and everything consumed amid a great haze'.

---

One night in 1716 the astronomer Halley witnessed an object so bright that he was able to read by its light

---

In March 1716 the great English astronomer Edmund Halley recorded seeing an object so intensely bright that it lit up the night sky as if it was day. Halley even noted that the light was so bright he could read a book by its glow.

In the Persian Gulf, on 15 May 1879, sailors aboard the British warship *Vulture* saw two giant, glowing objects in the sky. They described them as wheel-shaped, and claimed they spun slowly until descending almost to sea level. The mysterious objects were clearly visible to all, and seen for more than thirty minutes.

On 17 November 1882, the Greenwich Observatory reported seeing a large green disc hovering in the sky. Astronomers throughout Europe also reported viewing the object.

### THE TOP BRASS INVESTIGATE

The US government's involvement in the quest to authenticate or positively refute the existence of UFOs began in 1947, after the Arnold sighting. Senior military men first feared that the objects were secret Russian weapons. They threw a security cordon around their investigations, and passed off reported sightings as either simple misidentifications or the products of over-fertile imaginations.

But behind the closed doors of the Pentagon, the military brass was as baffled as anyone and set up a top-secret unit called Project Sign to look into the phenomena. Five years later, after a record number of sightings, the US Government set up Project Blue Book - another top-secret investigation.

According to the latest disclosures, it now seems apparent that it is still actively investigating mysterious, unexplained UFO encounters, despite years of official denials and ridicule of such sightings.

The government is secretly funding a massive investigation to determine if some UFO sightings are real, and decide once and for all if alien life is visiting the earth. Indeed, it has been reported that a top-secret panel, codenamed the UFO Working Group, is spending millions of dollars in the search, and has checked out dozens of spectacular sightings.

---

Cold War fears that the unexplained objects might be of Soviet military origin soon had to be laid aside

---

This Working Group is said to be an elite panel of military and civilian experts, which meets regularly in a

*Below:* **In the 1980s an English company had the idea of producing its own flying saucers which it hoped would eventually be able to carry cargo. This prototype was flown under radio control in a giant hangar in Bedfordshire.**

heavily guarded room deep inside the huge Pentagon complex. Their mission is simple: to determine if there is life out there in space.

One of the most fascinating, unsolved cases in the Group's files concerns a series of strange sightings - which had occurred many years earlier - over the small Wisconsin town of Elmwood.

Two undercover CIA operatives were sent in to test the validity of the sightings, and then threw a veil of secrecy over the probe as the government tried to contain it. 'One of the most impressive witnesses was policeman George Wheeler, a former World War combat flier,' said Howard Blum, a former correspondent for the *New York Times* and author of a book on the government's interest in UFOs. 'In April, 1975, Wheeler was patrolling the streets when he saw a huge ball of flame coming in the night sky. He raced after the object - and saw a craft, shaped like two cereal bowls together as big as a football field, hovering about 1500 feet above the ground. He reported that the strange craft took off at tremendous speed, performed amazing acrobatics and then disappeared in an instant.'

---

The US government takes the sightings so seriously that it has set up a top-secret working group to investigate them

---

A year later Officer Wheeler had a second encounter, this time observing a bright orange flame on the outskirts of the town. Thinking it was a fire in the distance, he radioed headquarters. Blum says when the officer got to the top of a small hill at the edge of town, he radioed: 'My God! It's one of those UFOs again. It's huge. As big as a two-storey house.'

The author said Wheeler described it as 'silver and 250 feet across, and a bright orange beam was coming from its domed roof'. Police chief Gene Helmer went to investigate the object, while his wife, Gail, manned the radio at headquarters.

'I'll never forget that night,' she said. 'George said he was looking at a UFO and it was obvious he was very excited.' As Wheeler described the craft to her it began to lift from the ground, then fired a

**Above:** *This apparent UFO, photographed over the mountains of the Polish-Czechoslovak border, has a simple explanation. It is, in fact, a cloud of a kind that does occasionally form over mountainous terrain.*

**Right:** *This UFO was said to have been photographed over the Clarence River in New Zealand.*

blue ray towards his squad car. 'He was knocked unconscious,' said Blum. 'And when he came to, he was in bad shape. He complained of severe pain in his arms and legs, and had severe headaches. He believed he was the victim of radiation poisoning from the ray. Before physicians could find a cause for his pain, he died suddenly.'

Although the US Government officially denies the existence of any top-secret UFO panel, it openly admits to an interest in searching for extraterrestrial life, which is no longer considered a scientific 'twilight zone'. In fact NASA has made the goal a priority.

---

As the police chief described the amazing sight over his radio, the craft fired a blue ray towards his squad car

---

The Space Agency's interest in the hunt for other intelligent life forms got a shot in the arm in 1988, when astronomers discovered that planetary systems were not confined to our own sun and nine orbiting planets, and that those distant relatives may also have given birth to life in some form. 'That is the circumstantial evidence that life

**Above:** *This photograph was taken by the manager of a photographic studio in Bulawayo, Zimbabwe.*

**Below:** *A somewhat hat-shaped UFO, photographed over a North American town.*

exists elsewhere,' said Michael Klein, a member of the NASA team.

For almost three decades, astronomers from Harvard and Ohio State University have been monitoring parts of the universe, hoping for that elusive radio signal. 'We've picked up quite a few strong signals, but they're never repeated,' said Skip Schwartz, a field station manager for the Harvard team. 'It's as frustrating as coming home to a ringing telephone. By the time you reach the receiver, the other party has hung up.'

### EXPERT WITNESSES

Millions of people around the world - from England to Australia to the United States to Russia - firmly believe the 'aliens' are already making limited contact. And there are some disturbing incidences of UFO sightings which even the experts cannot disclaim.

One of the most graphic sightings came on 15 August 1950, in Great Falls, Montana, when a local baseball team manager, Nicholas Mariana, and his secretary saw two brilliantly glowing objects appear over the park in broad daylight. The strange craft moved in unison across the sky.

---

One up on previous UFO witnesses, Nicholas Mariana had a home movie camera with him and managed to film his encounter

---

However, unlike previous witnesses to such encounters, Mariana had proof - he filmed more than 15 seconds of the spectacular aerial display with a 16mm home movie camera. The film, which is considered by UFO investigators as one

**Right:** *Another UFO sighting that was captured on film - this picture was taken from a car.*

**Below:** *Mrs Irmgard Lincoln hit the headlines in 1976 with her claims that Martians were planning to pay the United States a visit. Here she holds up photographs as 'proof' during a news conference.*

of the most impressive pieces of evidence ever gathered, shows two metal-like objects dancing across the sky.

In 1957, on a USAF training flight over the border between Mississippi and Texas, the crew of an RD-47 jet flying at 30,000 feet reported a radar signal

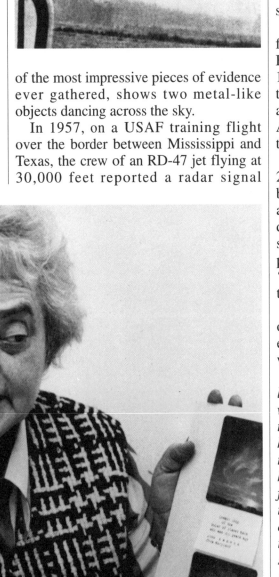

moving upwards on their screen. Both the captain and co-pilot then noticed a bright light heading towards them, and their sighting was confirmed by a radio report from the ground.

Twenty minutes later the pilot again saw the bright light, this time it was some 5000 feet below his plane - then, suddenly, the radar blip split in two. Seconds later, it was again one. The entire incident was later confirmed by a third installation, an air defence radar station in Duncanville, Texas.

There was no need for radar confirmation in an incident recorded over Boianai, in Papua New Guinea, in June 1959. Some thirty-eight people saw the two-day aerial display by several UFOs - and their inhabitants! - including an Anglican priest, William Gill, who had the good sense to make notes.

The first instance came on the night of 26 June, when Father Gill noticed a bright white light in the sky which appeared to be coming towards him. As it drew closer, he recalled it resembling a saucer-shaped disc, and being accompanied by several smaller objects. The 'mother-ship' was so bright that it lit up the night-time clouds.

The following night, a startled Gill and other witnesses were again privy to the encounter. 'We stood in the open to watch,' he wrote.

*Although the sun had set, it was quite light for the following fifteen minutes. We watched figures appear on top - four of them - there was no doubt they were human. Two smaller UFOs were seen at the same time, stationary, one over the hills, west, and one overhead. Two of the figures seemed to be doing something in the centre of the disk - they were occasionally bending over and raising their arms as though adjusting or setting something. One figure seemed to be standing, looking down on us.*

Could an Anglican priest have made up such a story? If so, why? And how could almost forty people witness the same strange incident?

And how could a highly trained Army helicopter pilot put his craft into a steep descent - only to find it climbing at more than 1000 feet a minute? That happened to Captain Larry Coyne on 18 October

1973, over Mansfield, Ohio, when he and three other crew members reported a near-collision with a UFO. It was shortly before 11pm when Coyne noticed a bright red light coming from the east, growing ever closer on what seemed to be a collision course.

---

When a highly trained Army helicopter crew reports being 'taken over' by a UFO, even the sceptics have to listen

---

The helicopter pilot estimated the UFO's speed at more than 600 knots and, with little time to spare, threw his craft into a steep dive to avoid a mid-air catastrophe. He looked up, and described the UFO as 'approximately 50 to 60 feet long, about as big as our aircraft. The leading edge of the craft was a bright red light. The trailing edge had a green light, and you could delineate where the light stopped and the gray metallic structure began. You could see because there were reflections of the red and green off the structure itself.'

Shortly afterwards, as the UFO broke off its 'surveillance' and disappeared into the night sky, Captain Coyne was startled to discover his helicopter was ascending, instead of descending. 'We were supposed to be going down,' he said. 'But we were going up!' Somehow, the alien craft had drawn the chopper upwards. Given the training and experience of the Army crew, the case caused a firestorm of controversy, but none of the four aviators ever changed their stories.

One of the most telling 'encounters' occurred in the early hours of 31 December 1978, over the South Island of New Zealand. An Australian television crew, retracing the flight path of several earlier planes whose crews had reported seeing strange, bright objects, actually filmed one of the mysterious lights.

The object, which also appeared on the plane's radar, was filmed on 16mm colour film, and could be clearly seen zipping through the night sky at speeds in excess of 3000 miles an hour.

The film caused a sensation, and was brought to the USA where scores of experts scrutinized it for signs of fakery or explainable phenomena. The team

**Above:** *UFO researchers Michael Lickman and Bill Knell claimed that aliens landed in the Queen's district of New York City in 1989.*

**Below:** *Vasya Surin from Voronezh in the former Soviet Union claimed that he had seen a UFO hovering over his home town in October 1989.*

unanimously agreed that it could not have been faked, or explained away in earthly terms.

EVEN CLOSER ENCOUNTERS

But visual sightings and radar confirmations of UFOs - no matter how incontrovertible - pale into insignificance when compared to stories of physical contact with extraterrestrials...stories often retold in stunning detail under hypnosis.

Certainly the most sensational account of such an encounter comes from a Brazilian farmer, Antonio Boas, who claims he might have fathered an extraterrestrial child. Boas, who was twenty-three at the time, told his incredible tale to Dr Olavo Fontes, who was treating him for what seemed to be radiation poisoning - a rare disorder for a farmer in the jungles of South America.

According to the deposition Dr Fontes recorded, the very close encounter occurred shortly after midnight on 15 October 1957. Boas was up late, ploughing a field on his tractor, when a

Above: *Frenchman Frank Fontaine went missing for several days in 1979. Later he claimed that he had been abducted by aliens in a UFO.*

'luminous, egg-shaped object' some twelve yards long and eight yards wide hovered over him briefly before landing in the paddock. The tractor engine and lights failed as the craft came to rest on three metal 'legs'. Suddenly four aliens, clad in helmets, descended from the object and dragged the stunned farmer up a ladder into the ship.

---

Brazilian farmer Antonio Boas claimed he was abducted by aliens and subsequently fathered an extraterrestrial child

---

Inside there were five aliens, whom Boas described as humanoid, and who spoke in 'a series of barks, slightly resembling the sounds made by a dog'. They were small, about five feet tall, and clad in 'very tight-fitting overalls'. He claims he was stripped naked, and blood

taken from his chin (Dr Fontes did indeed find two small scars on the farmer's chin during his examination).

Shortly afterwards, Boas recounted, a beautiful naked woman came into the room...and they made love. 'Shortly after we had separated,' he claimed, 'the door opened. One of the men appeared, and called the woman. Then she went out. But before going out she turned to me, pointed at her belly, and then pointed towards me and with a smile (or something like it), she finally pointed towards the sky.'

The best-known, and probably the most extensively documented, case of 'alien abduction' occurred thirty years ago, in Whitfield, New Hampshire. Barney and Betty Hill were on their way home to Portsmouth, New Hampshire, after a holiday in Canada. As they were driving south along US Route 3 late at night they saw a bright light moving erratically in the sky. Perplexed, they none the less drove on, although the light seemed to be following them. As they reached the White Mountains, the object, which had grown much larger, began to close in on them.

Barney stopped the car, and got out to observe the strange craft through a pair of binoculars. Incredibly, he saw up to eleven figures moving behind the rowed windows of the object. 'I don't believe it! I don't believe!' he repeated to his incredulous wife. He recalled the beings as humanoid, dressed in shiny black uniforms and visored caps.

By now, the UFO was less than twenty-five yards away, and Barney dashed back into the car, screaming: 'They are going to capture us!' He started the engine, and accelerated as fast as the vehicle would go...but suddenly the car began to shake, and the Hills lapsed into drowsiness. Two hours later, and some thirty-five miles away from where Barney had stopped the car, they regained total consciousness. They drove home, thoroughly bewildered by the experience and the 'missing' two hours.

For the next two years, they were plagued by nervous disorders and terrifyingly real dreams of being aboard an alien spaceship. Finally, unable to cope any longer with their anxiety, they visited Dr Benjamin Simon, a Boston psychiatrist who specialized in treating disorders through hypnotherapy.

For six months, beginning in January 1964, they were under the supervision of Dr Simon, and gradually their bizarre story came to light.

Both told identical tales of that night. Their car was stopped, and they were dragged out by a group of humanoids, less than five feet tall, with triangular heads and grey skin. Their eyes were large, slanted, and their mouths were nothing but tiny slits. Somehow, their language was translated into English in the Hills' minds. They took their two 'guinea pigs' aboard the craft, where they were given a thorough physical examination, then released.

---

**After sighting a UFO and its occupants they lost consciousness and woke up two hours later, thirty-five miles away**

---

However, Betty recalled something else - something which continues to amaze and baffle UFO experts. When she asked the 'leader' of the aliens where they were from, he pointed to a 'star map', which she later redrew under hypnosis. It wasn't until several years later, based on new astronomical data that was not available in 1961, that it was learned Betty had drawn an amazingly close map of a newly-discovered cluster of stars called Zeta Reticuli.

### SOVIET SIGHTINGS

While most of the more sensational accounts of UFO sightings and close encounters have been reported in the West, the advent of Glasnost in the former Soviet Union opened up a whole new world for UFO researchers.

Indeed, in 1989, the news agency, TASS reported that three aliens had visited a park in the city of Voronezh. Several residents told TASS that the visitors stood about 10 feet tall with 'very small heads'. A later report in the newspaper *Sovetskaya Kultura* added more details: One alien had 'three eyes, was clad in silvery overalls and boots the colour of bronze'. The creatures, TASS said, 'made a short promenade' around the park - accompanied by a small robot - before retreating to their spaceship.

These are a few among the growing numbers of people who claim to have seen UFOs or to have been abducted by their inhabitants. Does this mean that visitors from space are real? Or does it signal some form of mass hysteria? No one really knows. The answers may come in a generation, or tomorrow. Somewhere, up in that dark sky, there may be those who do know. But for now, mankind can only wait...and wonder.

**Below:** *The dramatic scenery of Hawaii forms a fitting setting for this alleged UFO sighting.*

# CAMELOT
## Arthur's Lost Court

The romantic tales of King Arthur and his Knights of the Round Table are familiar to most of us. Is it all the product of a storyteller's fertile imagination - or is there some truth behind the ancient legends?

*...'Tirra lirra', by the river*
*Sang Sir Lancelot.*
*She left the web, she left the loom,*
*She made three paces thro' the room,*
*She saw the water-lily bloom,*
*She saw the helmet and the plume,*
*She looked down to Camelot.*

The mystery and romance of Camelot, as captured in the epic poem by Alfred, Lord Tennyson, 'The Lady of Shalott', shows that in the nineteenth century, as in this one, the enduring mystery of King Arthur and his Knights of the Round Table had lost none of its

appeal. The legends of virtue, decency and manliness, are clung to by school-children and romantics, convinced that somewhere in the violent, disease-ridden and dangerous past that was pre-medieval England there existed a kingdom that flourished under the wise King and his righteous followers.

But is it all mere hocus-pocus, of the kind that might have been conjured up by the court wizard Merlin?

Was there an Excalibur, a Round Table, a Lady Guinevere and a Sir Lancelot? Or are these tales of fancy born in an age of despair to brighten up otherwise dismal lives?

### THE LEGEND IN LITERATURE

King Arthur and his court are referred to by scholars as the Arthurian Legend, and the first reference to the King seems to be in the epic Welsh poem *Gododdin*, which appeared around AD 600. In the poem, some tales are told of a 'mighty warrior'. Other early works show this mighty warrior as a Celtish chieftain who fought bravely against Saxon invaders of Britain.

In 1135, in *Historia*, Geoffrey of Monmouth mentioned King Arthur as the conqueror of western Europe, and afterwards Wace wrote another historical work called the *Roman De Bru*, which

imbued Arthur with the aura of chivalry and romance that has surrounded him ever since.

Then, in the next century, the French poet Chrestien de Troyes wrote five romances dealing with the knights of Arthur's court. His *Perceval* contains the earliest literary version of the most famous Arthurian odyssey, the quest for the Holy Grail, the chalice from which Christ is supposed to have drunk at the Last Supper.

---

The story of Perceval is the quest for the Holy Grail - the chalice from which Christ is said to have drunk at the Last Supper

---

Two medieval German poets were subsequently important for perpetuating the Arthur legend - Wolfram von Eschenbach and Gottfried von Strassburg, the latter writing the story of Tristan and Isolde. Sir Tristram was an Arthurian knight sent to Ireland to bring back Isolde the Fair to Cornwall to be the bride of his uncle, King Mark. The Cornish element in the story is important in later beliefs that the seat of King Arthur - Camelot - was in fact in the West Country.

After 1225 the legend seemed to grow thin with the Europeans, but it continued to thrive in Britain. *Sir Gawain and the Green Knight*, which appeared around

**Top:** *The Arthurian Legend was a favourite theme for Victorian artists - this painting depicts Sir Tristram being admitted into the fellowship of the Round Table.*

**Above:** *A 14th-century reconstruction of the Round Table from the Great Hall of Winchester Castle. It was painted for a visit by the Emperor Charles V in 1522.*

1370, is one of the best of all Middle English romances and fully embodies the romantic ideal of chivalry and honour.

That was followed by the last really important medieval work on the subject, *Morte d'Arthur*, by Sir Thomas Malory, whose tales became the source of many of the later Arthur tales.

No important works were written after this for several centuries until Tennyson's *Idylls of the King*. Later again, the German composer Richard Wagner used the Arthurian legends as the inspiration for many of his great operas.

## THE CELTIC MYTH

So, knowing that Arthur was written up as fable by a succession of writers, can there possibly be some foundation in fact? Most definitely yes, say those Arthurian Legend scholars who believe that only truth could have been the basis for such closely interwoven tales.

It is a truth founded not in English, but in Celtic, history. Research has shown that Arthurian legends were spread all over Europe by the twelfth century, broadcast by Breton minstrels from the north west French coast, whose dialect was - and is - remarkably similar to the now extinct Cornish language.

But before examining its roots, here is

what the Legend of King Arthur is all about. Arthur was the illegitimate son of Uther Pendragon, King of Britain, and his lover Igraine.

After Uther's death Arthur - who had been brought up in secrecy and was not known to his people - ascended the throne by declaring himself the rightful heir and withdrawing a mighty sword, Excalibur, from a block of stone. This was a feat that no pretender had been able to accomplish before him.

Merlin, the court wizard, then declared his parentage, bowed down before him and pronounced him King. Arthur reigned at Camelot and proved himself to be just, honest and decent, and evolved the egalitarian concept of a Round Table for his knights.

---

Arthur slew his arch-enemy Mordred, but, mortally wounded, was borne away to the magical Isle of Avalon

---

Arthur had several enemies including Morgan le Fay, his treacherous sister, and his nephew Mordred. Morgan was a sorceress and a schemer who plotted against Arthur for the throne. Mordred seized Arthur's throne while the King was away in battle.

In terrible combat King Arthur slew Mordred, but not before he was mortally

**Left:** *Sir Galahad, son of Sir Lancelot, and one of Arthur's most loyal followers.*

**Above left:** *Sir Gawain, Arthur's nephew, was the hero of one of the finest of medieval English romances - Sir Gawain and the Green Knight.*

**Above:** *The theme of chivalry has been a constant source of inspiration. This painting of a knight errant, by Sir John Gilbert, hangs in London's Guildhall.*

wounded himself. His body was borne away to the Isle of Avalon where it was said that his wounds would heal and from where his subjects believed he would have a second coming.

His two most devoted knights were Sir Tristram and Sir Lancelot of the Lake - who besmirched his chivalrous reputation by carrying on an affair with the Lady Guinevere, Queen of England and wife of Arthur.

Other knights included Sir Pelleas; Sir Gawain, Arthur's nephew; Sir Balin and Sir Balan; Sir Galahad, Lancelot's son; Sir Kay, Arthur's villainous foster-brother; Sir Percival, Sir Gareth, Sir Geraint and Sir Bedevere.

There are no historical records of such people, nor of a court of Camelot, nor of a king who ruled England with bene-volence and chivalry. But back in the mists of time, among the fierce tribes of Wales, it is believed that the legend was born out of reality.

## THE HISTORICAL REALITY

Eminent Arthurian scholar Alfred Nutt, in *Studies on the Legend of the Holy Grail,* and Professor Sir John Rhys, in his *Studies in the Arthurian Legend,* theorize that the King was born in Celtic folklore based on tribal leaders. The earliest Celts, who arrived in Britain in about 500 BC, were called Goidels and came from Gaul. It is from these hardy, warlike people that the Arthurian Legend stems.

In AD 410 Rome gave notice that internal problems in Italy made it impossible for her troops to govern any longer and so, after 360 years of occupation, they were withdrawn. With the Romans gone the land became a battlefield, invaded by Saxon raiders, Jutes and Angles, while Picts and Scots teemed over the deserted Hadrian's Wall.

It was in this time of turmoil that, in 443, an appeal was made to Rome for assistance. It fell on deaf ears. The bold Scots and Picts forayed as far south as Kent where they drove the Kentish chief, a Celt called Vortigern, to desperation. Too tired for war, he fled westwards to Wales and built himself a citadel.

Determined to make it impregnable, Vortigern consulted his magicians and soothsayers. They advised him to sacrifice an orphan child and bury it in the foundations of his fortress. The boy he chose, Ambrosius, son of a Roman couple of consular rank, saved himself by displaying a gift for prophecy.

This is fact - but the legend goes on to say that the boy was Myrddin, Welsh for Merlin. Others believe that the citadel may have been the Camelot of legend.

Nennius, a ninth-century historian, wrote that a descendant of Vortigern fell at the Battle of Mount Badon fighting the Saxons. Historians have searched ever since for Mount Badon, and suggestions

**Below:** *King Arthur bids farewell to his beloved Guinevere in a convent. She conducted an affair with Sir Lancelot behind Arthur's back.*

as to its whereabouts include Bath, Badbury near Swindon and Badbury Hill near Farringdon. Some theorize that this descendant may have been King Arthur.

In the twelfth century, as King Arthur fever gripped the imagination of a wretched peasantry, the remains of a Celtic man and a woman were found within the walls of Glastonbury Abbey. This, said the monks at the time, was the Avalon of legend, and they had found King Arthur and his wife Guinevere, who had been buried there at a later date.

## There were many links between the Arthurian legends and the details of Celtic history

The Celtic connection has parallels with many of the details in the Arthur stories. The Round Table, for instance, was typical in Celtic communities where the tribal elders sat in a circle with the chieftain in his 'seat perilous' - he had to be challenged in combat for his seat to be taken by another. The Holy Grail may have been based upon the simple drinking vessels used by the Celts.

The battle at which Arthur died, called the Battle of Camlann, may have been fought near Cadbury in Somerset, and countless excavations and man hours have gone into examining the area - without much luck. Finally, the Celtic religion played an important part in Celtic life, and certainly the Arthur of legend was a devoted Christian and 'defender of the faith'.

So fact or fiction, myth or memory? American Arthurian scholar James Dunsford suggests:

*The King Arthur we know in Hollywood mythology and English folk-lore was very different from the real King Arthur, who represented strong ideals in a bad world. But I am convinced that there is indeed something in these stories and that Camelot did exist, as did the knights, or warriors who served him. But it was an age when nothing was recorded, nothing preserved. I venture that one day we may have more concrete evidence than this, but until then King Arthur will be more widely remembered as a story than as a reality.*

# CORN CIRCLES
## Mysteries of the Fields

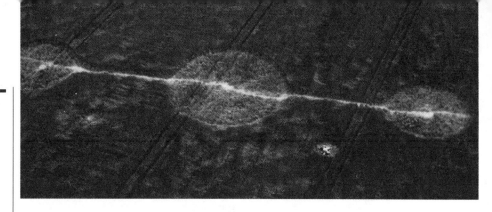

# The great corn circle debate began centuries ago. Now it has gripped the imagination of the public and the press. Are these strange phenomena created by freak weather conditions, aliens from outer space - or hoaxers?

**P**ractical jokers, whirlwinds, hedgehogs, mating foxes or Unidentified Flying Objects...everyone has a theory about the unexplained phenomenon of corn circles. It is a mystery that caused a stir throughout the eighties but which burst afresh into the public eye with a rash of sightings at the start of the nineties. The mainly elliptical circles varied from 10ft to 200ft and more in diameter. More than a thousand circles, some surrounded by up to four outer rings, were recorded in a handful of English counties between 1980 and 1990. Although flattened, the crop was not damaged and the curves had an unnerving neatness to them.

---

### In the late seventeenth century fairies and the devil were still under serious consideration as causes

---

Scientists, meteorologists and farmers came up with an astonishing array of explanations for the seemingly instant appearances of these circles and other patterns in fields of crops. A £10,000 reward was even offered by a British national newspaper. But the mystery went unsolved.

While all this was going on, what no one seemed to appreciate was that the crop circle phenomenon was not entirely 'news'. In fact, the riddle taxed great minds three hundred years ago and more.

In 1686 Robert Plot, Professor of Chemistry at Oxford University, wrote a book called *The Natural History of Staffordshire*. In it he searched for some 'higher principle' to explain crop circles rather than the current theories such as rutting deer, urinating cattle and fairies.

Professor Plot did not entirely debunk such myths, saying that 'the Fairies so much tak't about' might indeed be to blame. He wrote: 'They may indeed

**Above:** *A couple caught 'making hay' in a corn circle. Not the answer to the mystery!*

**Opposite:** *Corn circles began to be reported in great numbers in 1980.*

**Below:** *Although flattened, crops are rarely damaged.*

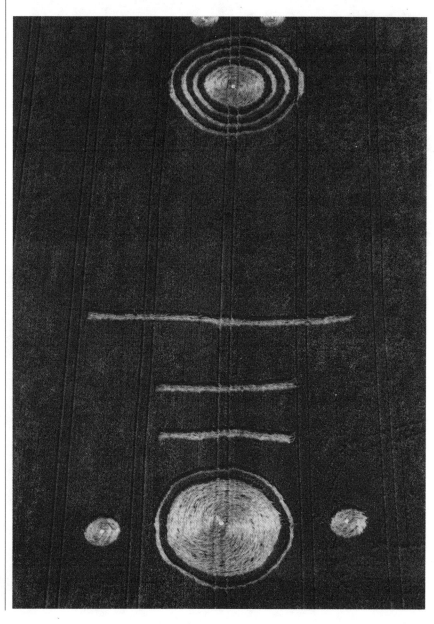

occasion such circles', but added that the repetitive plodding of animals was a far more believable cause.

However, after intense deliberation, Professor Plot concluded: 'They must needs be the effects of lightning, exploded from the clouds most times in a circular manner.'

The pent-up energy would be emitted from the cloud 'so as at due distance to become a circle and in that forme to strike the Earth'.

And what about the crop marks that were not circular? That was due to the fact that sometimes lightning got forced out of clouds in a rectangular shape!

**Below:** *A pamphlet published in 1678 blamed Satan for crop circles.*

**Bottom:** *In the 1980s, the theory that UFOs were behind crop circles was the most widely discussed.*

## CONFLICTING MODERN THEORIES

Why then did the whole crop circle debate go dormant for almost three centuries afterwards? Fewer explanations are offered here than for the corn circles themselves. But it was certainly true that, until the eighties, the crop circle argument had been less than lively. Then, when more and more people began reporting sightings, a whole array of suggestions were put forward to capture the imagination of the public.

---

For three hundred years the debate lay dormant, ignored by scientists and public alike

---

In place of fairies and devils, UFOs became the most popular explanation. Mating animals was also a suggestion. So was the theory that hedgehogs had been driven to circular motion by dementia. Another theory voiced was that aliens had decided to communicate through the Sumerian sign language of tribesmen who lived around the borders of Iraq some five thousand years ago.

Perhaps not so strange was that the theories most favoured by scientists were those linked to weather conditions.

Consultant meteorologist Dr Terence Meaden, head of the Tornado and Storm

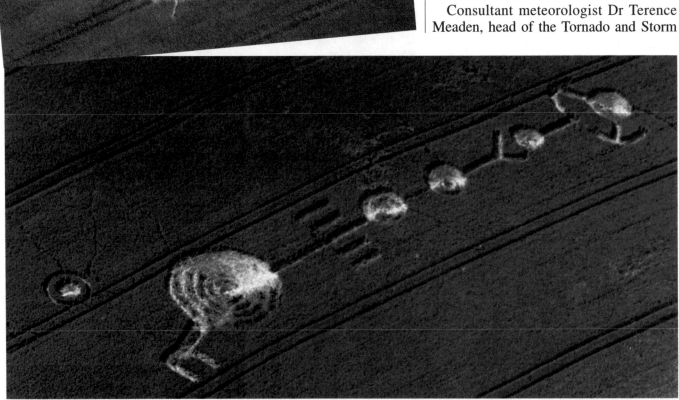

Research Organization believed that other weather conditions - and wind energy in particular - were a factor.

He announced to a conference at Oxford Polytechnic in 1988 that the mystery had been solved. He told his audience that the circles were formed by sudden whirlwinds. Most of the circles were formed near hillsides, the explanation being that wind gusts on only one side of a hill, creating vortexes of gyrating air which move suddenly downwards to create the circles.

---

Have demented hedgehogs run in circles, or is something from 'out there' communicating in an archaic Middle Eastern sign language?

---

Another leading investigator, Colin Andrews, disagrees with the whirlwind theory. In 1983 he and his team of eleven scientific colleagues set out to research phenomena in central southern England.

Reporting their findings in 1989, he and his team ruled out hoaxers, aliens, helicopters and whirlwinds. They said they believed that unprecedented atmospheric conditions caused by the newly discovered hole in the earth's ozone layer were to blame for the farmland phenomena.

Andrews, an electrical expert with the local authority in the Test Valley in Hampshire, said: 'We now believe that the shifts in the earth's electromagnetic conditions caused by the ozone hole may be responsible. One of the circles that appeared recently in Hampshire amazed

**Above:** *Meteorologist Dr Terence Meaden claimed in 1988 that whirlwinds caused such precise patterns as this.*

**Below:** *In 1989 a team of investigators cited atmospheric complications caused by the depleted ozone layer as the cause of crop circles.*

us even more than the others because the flattened crops grew back in a dartboard formation. There were seven concentric rings of crops, with a series of perfect spokes going out from the centre.'

After a later discovery of a vast formation of crop circles and other patterns, a worried Colin Andrews said that the molecular structure of some of the plants had been changed. He said: 'We have written to the Ministry of Agriculture asking them to take the affected crops out of circulation. It is possible that molecular contamination has taken place.'

On another major investigation, Mr Andrews and his partner Pat Delgado borrowed equipment from the Army to keep lengthy surveillance on fields likely to be affected. They reported that the circles were being caused by 'some form of higher intelligence'.

---

Some scientists believe the phenomenon may be caused by the recent hole in the earth's ozone layer

---

Andrews said: 'They are caused by some sort of high energy but we don't know what. The shapes are becoming more and more complex and I believe that what we are heading for is circles in the form of snowflakes or flowers. The shapes we have seen recently are just the start of what is to come.'

The crop circle debate has tended to centre on southern England. But similar markings have been reported from North America, Australia and Japan. Japanese scientists who visited Britain to investigate the phenomenon have taken the ozone layer theory seriously. But they have come up with other explanations.

Professor Yoshihiko Ohtsuki, from Tokyo's Waseda University, said in 1991: 'The circles are caused by an elastic plasma, which is a very strong form of ionized air. In an experiment...we created a plasma fireball which, if it touched a plate covered in aluminium powder, created beautiful circles and rings, just like the ones seen in fields.'

### AN UNNERVING EXPERIENCE

On a sunny August day that same year a couple out for a walk found themselves in the middle of a crop circle in the making. It was the first time that anyone

**Above:** *Some people have put forward the theory that crop circles are signs left by aliens using an ancient Middle Eastern language.*

**Below:** *A crop circle in Wiltshire, one of the two English counties most affected by the phenomenon.*

had found themselves with first-hand knowledge of how the circles are created.

Gary and Vivienne Tomlinson, of Guildford in Surrey, were strolling along a footpath at the edge of a Hampshire cornfield when the crop started moving...the couple were being caught in the eye of a brand-new corn circle.

Vivienne Tomlinson recalled:

*There was a tremendous noise. We looked up to see if it was caused by a helicopter but there was nothing. We felt a strong wind pushing us from the side and above. It was forcing down on our heads - yet incredibly my husband's hair was standing on end. Then the whirling air seemed to branch into two and zig-zag off into the distance. We could still see it like a light mist or fog, shimmering as it moved. As it disappeared we were left standing in a corn circle with the corn flattened all around us. Everything became very still again and we were left with a tingly feeling.*

Husband Gary added: 'We didn't speak for ages, and we told no one about the incident until three days later.'

---

It was three days before the Tomlinsons could bring themselves to tell anyone what had happened

---

When the Tomlinsons did eventually speak of their experience, Dr Terence Meaden immediately took them back to the site, near Hambledon. He reported: 'There is a perfectly logical explanation for this. It is that when a strong gust of wind blows over a hill, it rushes into the still air on the other side and causes a spiralling column.'

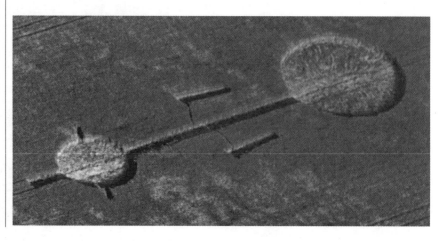

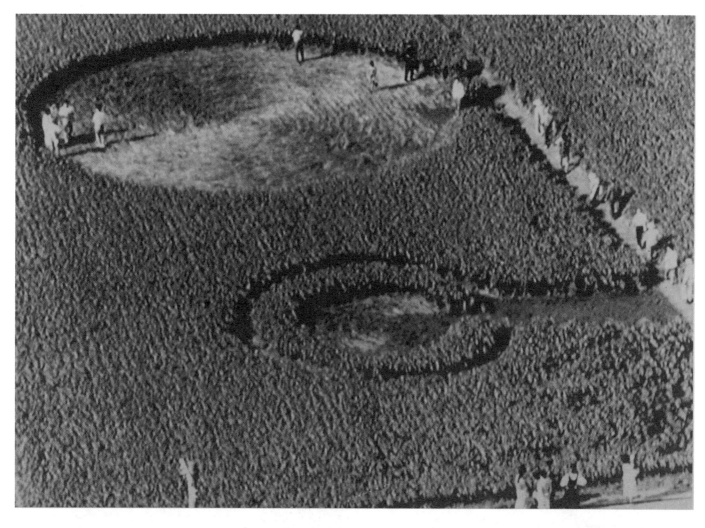

### HOAX OR GENUINE?

The summer of 1991 was a vintage period for corn circles. Circles even appeared on farmland at the Prime Minister's country retreat, Chequers. The local who found them said: 'If they were made by humans it is extraordinary that the perpetrators were not caught by security men guarding the Prime Minister.'

---

**If the circles at Chequers were made by humans, it seems odd that security guards noticed nothing**

---

The most extraordinary sighting, however, was one reported by Eddie Wise, of Bristol, who spent four nights in a Wiltshire field trying to solve the mystery...and claims he saw an alien spacecraft land. He said: 'It was enormous. There were no lights but I could see what appeared to be windows. A long object was lowered from the base of the craft and when it touched down in the field everything became quite still.'

Some British farmers were upset by the rash of corn circles. Each one, on average, costs them £60 in damaged crops, they say. Others cashed in on the boom, however. Suddenly signs sprang up outside farm gates, offering parking facilities for passers-by who wished to visit sites.

Are the crop patterns created in recent years no more than elaborate middle-of-the-night hoaxes? It has always been obvious that many of them were hoaxes - the work of elaborate practical jokers.

Indeed in 1991, two British artists, Dave Chorley and Doug Bower, claimed to have created all the major corn circles found over the previous thirteen years. They claimed to have fooled Japanese scientists, farming organizations and government departments. Using poles, boards and ropes, they recreated a corn circle in a field in Kent. It fooled the experts...but failed to silence the debate.

**Above:** *Even ancient man was mystified by crop circles, believing they were a sign from the heavens. We are not much wiser today.*

# YETIS
# Tracks in the Snow

Hairy beasts, half-ape, half-man, have long been reported from Siberia, the Himalayas and western North America. What lies behind the legends of the Chinese Wildman, the Abominable Snowman and Bigfoot?

The International Society of Cryptozoology in Tucson, Arizona, has only about three hundred members - but is the subject of a great deal of cynical comment. The reason is the strange work of the organization.

'Cryptozoology researches sightings of strange creatures,' says the society's secretary, anthropologist Richard Greenwell. 'It also studies a culture's literature and folklore of reports of strange creatures that may not be known to scientists.'

In short, Mr Greenwell and his fellows believe in monsters. And to admit that Bigfoot or the Wildman of China actually exists is to leave oneself open for a bit of mickey-taking.

If the pygmy elephant is a recent zoological discovery, why shouldn't the Abominable Snowman turn out to be genuine too?

It is only when recently collated evidence is studied that many laymen too begin to believe in the unbelievable. A number of new species of beast have already been discovered, say the cryptozoologists. Among them are the pigmy elephant of central Africa, which is one third the size of a normal elephant, and the onza, a fierce variety of mountain lion which had been legendary for years among Mexican peasants.

The pigmy hippopotamus, the white rhinoceros, the giant panda and the komodo dragon are other examples of

**Above:** *A recent reconstruction of the hairy creature of the Far East - variously called a Yeti, Wildman of China, Meti, Yeren and Abominable Snowman.*

**Opposite:** *The blurred outline of one of the Yeti's cousins, the Sasquatch or Bigfoot, running through the forests of Oregon, North America.*

**Left:** *The indefatigable traveller and explorer Sir Francis Galton, whose interests included the study of strange and unusual species.*

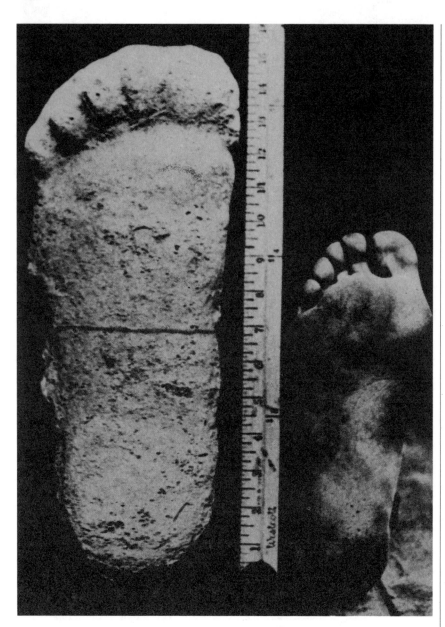

**Above:** *Plaster cast of a Bigfoot's tracks found in North America, compared with the size of a human foot.*

discoveries of hitherto unknown wildlife. 'These bizarre animals were proved not to be the stuff of imagination,' says Richard Greenwell. 'So why should there not be even more mysterious creatures out there?'

Among these, three wild creatures have gripped the imaginations of ordinary people more than any others. The reason could be that reports describe them as half-man, half-beast.

These creatures are known variously as Bigfoot, Sasquatch, Shookpa, Alma, Meti, Yeti, Abominable Snowman, Kang-mi, Migo, Yeren and the Wildman of China. Few scientists took reported sightings of these animals too seriously until recent evidence arose from an unexpected source...

## THE WILDMAN OF CHINA

Sightings of a creature the Chinese call the Yeren have been made by peasants over the centuries. A man-like primate with human features, the Yeren (or Wildman of China) stands 6ft tall and may possess toolmaking and basket-weaving ability. Hundreds of sightings by farming folk in central China were largely ignored by scientists. But recent hair samples may prove that the creature really does exist.

Until the late eighties, Western scientists had not been allowed access to the desolate forest area where a wealth of evidence about the monster had been collected by Chinese researchers. Then six countries, including Britain and the United States, invested £250,000 to send a team to the region to look at the evidence and bring back hair samples for high-technology analysis.

Gene Poirier, professor of anthropology at Ohio State University, was one of those who, like Richard Greenwell, was persuaded to travel to central China to collect data on the existence of a forest version of the Himalayan Yeti. What they uncovered was the most exciting find of their lives.

Poirier himself was a reluctant hunter. As a renowned scientist, he had always dismissed reports of such a beast. But his teaming up with Englishman Greenwell led to a fascinating two-year quest. And an independent London television film-maker, Geraldine Easter, was there with her camera team to record the evidence.

Sophisticated analysis of a few hairs proved the existence of a hitherto unknown higher primate

Evidence of the creature's existence consisted mainly of hair samples collected by farmers who had seen the monster on their land. Shanghai's Fudan University first discovered that the samples were from neither a man nor an ape. Yet they were certainly animal hairs.

The hairs were then sent to Ohio State University and to England's Birmingham University, where work was carried out by the Department of Space Research and Physics under Dr Rangeet Sokhi. The results of the tests were announced in November 1990. The scientists' conclusion was dramatic. The samples were from a creature which was neither man nor ape...which proved that the Wildman of China actually existed.

As further tests began to analyse the structure of the hair's chromosomes, the basic structures of life, Professor Poirier said: 'We have established that the animal does not fall into any known category. This is the first evidence of the existence of a new higher primate.'

The latest breakthrough from central China suggests that a creature called Gïgantopithecus, which existed half a million years ago - long before man - has managed to survive in extremely remote areas. Jawbones and more than a thousand teeth of this early 'ape man' have been found across China, and Vietnam and India.

Geraldine Easter says: 'The Chinese Wildman is either a beast we know nothing of or he is Gigantopithecus, which has somehow managed to beat extinction in these areas alone. He was a contemporary of the panda bear - and pandas have survived.'

### EYE-WITNESS ACCOUNTS

In 1981 the China Wildman Investigation and Research Society was established in Hubei province. Among the eye-witness reports collected by the society are these:

*On the morning of 19 June 1976 Gong Yulan, a woman farmer from Qunli village in Fangxian county's Qiaoshang township, went into the mountains with her four-year-old child to cut grass for her pigs. As she climbed a strip of land between the hills she suddenly noticed a reddish-brown creature was scratching its back against a tree only six or seven metres away. When the creature saw Gong Yulan and her child it rushed towards them. Gong fled down the mountain and later described the creature to the investigation group. She said it was taller than an adult human at 1.8 metres. The hair on its head was comparatively long and both its hands and feet were hairy. It walked erect like a human and it took long strides. It was a*

*male and its appearance terrified her. When she was shown a photograph of an erect orang-utan, Gong said: 'It looked just like this.' When she was shown photos of a bear, she shook her head.*

---

A Chinese peasant woman, shown a photo of an orang-utan, said the creature that had scared her looked just like it

---

Zhu Guoqiang, a stockman from Huilong township in Fangxian county, gave this evidence:

*On 16 June 1974 I was herding four oxen over a ridge at Longdonggou when I suddenly came face to face with a creature resembling a human but covered with brown hair. I aimed my gun at it but it grabbed the barrel. I pulled and pushed but I couldn't make it let go, so I fired anyway but missed. It opened its mouth wide, making a frightening face and showing its yellow teeth, which were similar to a human's but a bit wider. My legs turned to jelly. Three of the oxen had moved away but a large black bull, which had previously gored people, snorted and rushed at the creature as it stood still*

**Below:** *Rant Mullens from Washington State with wooden replicas of a Wildman's feet. He had carved them from wood.*

*clutching the end of my rifle. The beast dropped the gun and ran away.*

In the Qinling Mountains in north-west China, in the early 1950s, Fan Jingquan was working as part of a geological prospecting team for the Ministry of Heavy Industry. During his two-year contract he met many locals who had seen Wildmen and who had even fed them. He persuaded one old man to take him to a chestnut grove where the creatures roamed. This is his story:

---

The young male Wildman showed no fear, and ran up to the old man to take the chestnuts he was carrying

---

*As expected, a creature arrived. She was at least 1.6 metres tall and had a young one with her. Maybe because my clothes were different to the old man's she seemed particularly wary of me. But the young boy creature was fearless, running up to the old man for the chestnuts he was carrying. The mother called it back. The sound she made was neither like a horse nor a donkey.*

Zhang Yujin, from Hongta township in Fangxian county, once helped kill a Wildman. He says:

*I was eighteen years old and an orderly in the local Kuomintang army cadre. In the spring of 1943 I was with a hunting group of fifty or sixty soldiers when we came across a house in the hills. The owner told us that a creature had been crying on the slopes behind the house for half a day. The county magistrate, who was leading our hunt, ordered myself and another thirty soldiers to take three machine guns and surround the place. But when we arrived we saw not one but two creatures. One was sitting down with its head lowered and crying. The other was walking round the first and touching it every now and then. We watched for half an hour and then opened fire. The one that had been walking fled immediately and the other fell dead. When we examined it we found it was male, as tall as a human and its entire body was covered in dark red hair.*

---

Many tales of the Chinese Wildmen speak of tears rolling down their cheeks

---

Tales of the crying Wildmen have a common theme. Liu Jikuan told investigators how she had seen a captured pair of creatures paraded in 1942.

*I was thirteen that year and went to the centre of town to see the strange monsters which had been captured by the Kuomintang army and were tied up with a chain. They were a male and female. Their heads were bigger than a human's and their hair hung down to their shoulders. The female had big breasts and the male had tears rolling down its cheeks. We gave them an ear of corn and they ate it.*

This sort of evidence is easy to question. The eye-witnesses tend to be peasants and the antiquity of their stories arouses suspicion of embellishment. But recent provincial expeditions in the Chinese hinterland have been carried out in a thoroughly scientific manner.

Recently the Department of Biology at Huadong University organized several expeditions which collected first-hand evidence of Wildman footprints, caves, hair and 'nests' - strangely woven wooden constructions, sometimes assembled dozens at a time, and assumed to be the homes of the Wildmen.

**Below:** *Supposed Yeti footprints. A belief in the Yeti is still fairly widespread among Tibetans.*

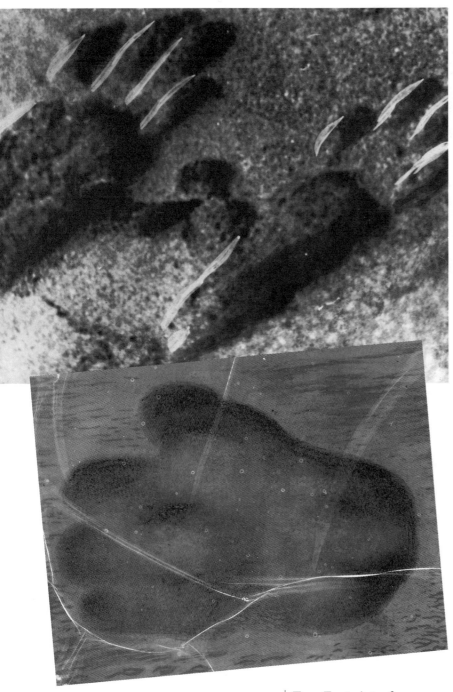

perhaps the large langur monkey. But in a scientific journal Hodgson described how some Nepalese porters had 'fled in terror' from an erect, tail-less creature with shaggy hair that ambled up to them.

They called it a *rakshas*, the Sanskrit word for 'demon'. They told him that references to Wildmen went back to the fourth century BC.

Half a century went by before another Briton, Major Lawrence Waddell of the Indian Army Medical Corps, reported seeing remarkable footprints which were 'said to be the trail of one of the hairy men who live in the eternal snows'. He discovered the tracks 17,000 ft up in north-east Sikkim.

---

**Reports from remote regions are often dismissed as the exaggerations of superstitious peasants**

---

In his book *Among the Himalayas* he wrote: 'The belief in these creatures is universal among Tibetans. None, however, of the Tibetans I have interrogated on the subject could ever give me an authentic case.'

In his conclusion, Waddell insisted that the hairy Wildmen were simply vicious, meat-eating, yellow snow bears that frequently preyed upon yaks.

The next recorded sighting of tracks by a European was in 1914 when J.R.P. Gent, a British forestry officer stationed in Sikkim, wrote of discovering footprints of what must have been a huge and amazing creature.

The sightings sparked worldwide curiosity, and mountaineers headed for the area in strength throughout the 1920s and 30s. They returned home with even more details of the astonishing Yeti. It was at this time that a newspaper reporter coined the phrase 'Abominable Snowman' to describe the beast.

Nepalese villagers, Tibetan lamas and the hardy sherpas had plenty of stories to tell. They told visitors that Yetis had always lived along the snow line that separates the wooded lower slopes from the desolate, icy wastes above.

Reports differed. Some said the animals were anything up to 12 ft high but extremely agile. Others described the

## THE ABOMINABLE SNOWMAN

The Wildman of China came to Western attention only in recent years. But across the Himalayas lives a creature whose existence was first reported to the West way back in 1832.

An adventurous Briton, B.H. Hodgson, went to live with the Nepalese high in the mountains and wrote home about a tall, erect, ape-like creature covered in thick hair. In Britain, it was assumed that the imaginative adventurer was mistakenly referring to the Himalayan red bear or

**Top:** *Footprints of an Abominable Snowman which appeared in western Sikkim. Other marks on the photo were made by the party that discovered them.*

**Above:** *Simulation of a footprint found in the Himalayas by the explorer Eric Shipton in 1951.*

**Above:** *This 1955 picture shows a Nepalese official holding a large animal's scalp, kept at Thangboche monastery for about a century.*

One villager's report of the time said:

*On catching sight of us, he stood up to his full height. He was very tall and lean, over six feet, and dressed in deerskin. He had a mop of unkempt hair and very long arms. His face was as big as a human's but his forehead was small and protruded over his eyes like the peak of a cap. His chin was large and broad, far bigger than a human's. Other than being a little taller, he was very much like a human. The next moment he ran away. He ran very fast, leaping high after every third step, and he was barefoot.*

---

Siberian villagers went on a berry-picking expedition and discovered a strange hairy creature which had had the same idea

---

But how much of this was hearsay? It was very difficult to find hard proof for the existence of an Abominable Snowman. Tibetan lama monasteries were rumoured to have scalps, skins and even mummified bodies of the creatures, but no Westerners had been able to get their hands on any of these bizarre relics to bring them back home for analysis.

Then in 1921 Colonel C.K. Howard-Bury became the first European ever to see a real live Yeti...

The colonel was heading a British expedition attempting to climb the world's highest mountain in the first Everest Reconnaissance Expedition. He and his team were clambering over a ridge some 21,000 feet up when they spotted a strange group of creatures on the Lhapka-La Pass.

The sherpas immediately jumped to the conclusion that this must 'the wild man of the snows' When they reached the spot where the creatures had been, they discovered huge footprints in the snow, 'each of them about three times the size of a human print'.

On his return to Britain, Howard-Bury read up on the ways and customs of the Himalayan 'wild man'. He discovered that naughty Tibetan children were threatened into behaving themselves with warnings about the massive creature.

Said Howard-Bury: 'The children are told that to escape from the creature they

creature as walking with its head held high but with a lolloping gait, its long arms swinging by its sides.

Villagers said the creatures were shy and only approached areas of human habitation when hunger forced them to do so. Their diet was mainly rodents and lichen, and they disembowelled their prey before consuming it - a peculiarly human trait. Furthermore, said the villagers, a Yeti would make a distinctive yelping sound when scared.

This, then, was the Abominable Snow-man as described by local inhabitants. But where was proof of his existence?

### FROM HEARSAY TO PROOF

In the 1920s a Chuchunna (a name meaning 'outcast' given to the man-beast in the Yakutiya region of eastern Siberia) was seen by villagers. The creature was picking berries, and stuffing them into its mouth with both hands.

have to run very fast down the hill because then his long hair falls over his eyes and he can't see them.' He also learned that the females of the species were hampered by the size of their breasts. One sherpa reported: 'We followed the track of two female Yeti and their breasts were so large they had to throw them over their shoulders before they could bend down.'

---

Female Yetis, said the sherpas, had to throw their massive breasts over their shoulders before they could bend down

---

In the spring of 1925 a sighting was made by British photographer N.A. Tombazi. He observed one of the elusive creatures 50,000 feet up the Zemu Glacier and, since he was a Fellow of the Royal Geographical Society, his testimony was not be laughed at.

In his book *Bigfoot* - the name later associated with the ape-like creatures of North America - John Napier quotes Tombazi as follows:

*Unquestionably the figure in outline was exactly like a human being...It showed up dark against the snow and, as far as I could make out, wore no clothes. Within the next minute or so it had moved into some thick scrub and was lost to view. Such a fleeting glimpse, unfortunately, did not allow me to set the telephoto camera, or even to fix the object carefully with my binoculars. But a couple of hours later, during the descent, I purposely made a detour so as to pass the place where the 'man' or 'beast' had been seen. I examined the footprints which were clearly visible on the surface of the snow.*

In 1936 the expedition of Ronald Kaulback confirmed the widespread existence of mysterious footprints. A year later the first photograph allegedly showing a Yeti's footprint was taken by Frank Smythe.

During World War II, five Polish prisoners being held in a Siberian labour camp escaped from their Soviet captors and made an incredible march across Mongolia and Tibet to Bhutan where, in

**Below:** *Thangboche monastery at the foot of Mount Everest in the Himalayas has been the base for many mountaineering expeditions - and the source of many yeti reports.*

1942, they crossed the Himalayas to India. They recounted a strange episode which had occurred in the mountains.

They said they had looked down from a ledge and spotted two burly ape-men only a few feet below them. The creatures were aware that they were being observed but showed no emotion and, seemingly ignoring the strangers, continued to shuffle through the snow.

---

**Prisoners escaping from a Siberian labour camp watched a pair of Yetis at close range for over two hours**

---

This was just another story which intrigued Yeti followers throughout the world. But the only real evidence was still the 1937 photograph. No first-hand evidence about the Abominable Snowman had yet been obtained.

### HARD EVIDENCE

On 8 November 1951, however, all that was to change. Mountaineer Eric Shipton was climbing with fellow Briton Michael Ward and Sherpa Sen Tensing in the Gauri Sankar range. They came across a trail of crystal-clear footprints 18,000 ft up on the Men-lung Glacier.

The marks were made by a flat-footed creature with five toes, one much bigger than the rest. The prints measured 13 in long and 8 in across, indicating a creature no less than 8 ft tall.

The photographs and Shipton's impeccable knowledge - he was an expert on footprints - just had to be believed. And the search for the Abominable Snowman attracted new interest.

Then, in 1952, the mighty Everest mountain was finally conquered by New Zealander Edmund Hillary and Sherpa Tensing Norgay. Although Hillary found giant prints too, he remained sceptical about the existence of the Yeti. But he was later to mount an expedition investigating the existence of the creature and how man adapted to life in extremely high altitudes. The expedition ended with Sir Edmund returning clutching a Snowman scalp which he had come across at the Khumjung monastery. Zoologists classified it as a goat antelope.

In 1957 Texas oilman Thomas Slick took up the trail. He and his party found tracks that Nepalese villagers said had been made by Yetis which had killed five people in that area. But no sign of the creatures was spotted on this expedition.

British mountaineer Don Whillans spent a day in 1970 photographing strange footmarks 13,000 ft up in the mountains of Nepal. That night, he said, the light of the moon allowed him to see clearly an ape-like creature bounding on all fours along a nearby ridge.

In 1978, Sir John (now Lord) Hunt, who had led the original Hillary-Tensing assault on Everest, returned to Nepal with Lady Hunt to commemorate the twenty-fifth anniversary of the 1953 ascent. They saw and photographed large tracks in the snow right outside their huts. Lord Hunt also related a story told him by the abbot of Thangboche monastery about his encounter with a Yeti.

---

**When the monks blew on conch shells and horns, the intruding Yeti ambled quietly away**

---

*This beast, loping along sometimes on his hind legs and sometimes on all fours, stood about five feet high and was covered with grey hair. The Yeti stopped to scratch, picked up some snow, played with it and made a few grunts. Instructions were given to ward off the unwelcome visitor. Conch shells were blown and the long, traditional horns sounded. The Yeti ambled away...*

Further clues to the Abominable Snowman can certainly be found in remote monasteries of Tibet. But following a Communist takeover, Tibet has become inaccessible to foreigners.

### BIGFOOT

More accessible however - although in many ways even more mysterious - are the forests and mountains making up the wilderness that covers the entire west coast of North America. Throughout that wild terrain lurk creatures of no known species. Yet over the years they have become widely known, and been given the familiar name of Bigfoot.

In 1851 the first recorded newspaper report of such a creature was published. Strangely, it was not a report from the West Coast, where most Bigfoot sightings have since been made, but in Greene County, Arkansas. This 'animal bearing the unmistakable likeness of humanity' was thought to be a 'survivor of the earthquake which devastated the area in 1811'. The creature was seen chasing a herd of cattle.

---

**The Arkansas Bigfoot was observed chasing cattle - the Himalayan Yeti is said to be a menace to yak herds**

---

No less an eminence than President Theodore Roosevelt recounted another early Bigfoot sighting. In 1903 the president, a keen hunter, retold the story of two trappers in the Salmon River district of Idaho who were attacked by a mysterious creature.

In 1924 came the most dramatic encounter with a Bigfoot so far recounted. Albert Ostman, also a lumberman, from Langley, British Columbia, said he had been camping opposite Vancouver Island when he was snatched by a giant Bigfoot. Ostman said the beast picked him up, still in his sleeping bag, and carried him 'like a sack of potatoes' for approximately three hours to its lair.

As dawn broke, Ostman realized that he was being held by four Bigfeet - male and female adults, and a pair of male and female children. He still had his rifle with him, but was reluctant to use it since the ape-like family had done him no harm. He also still had a few cans of food and other provisions that were buried in his sleeping bag. These he consumed while in captivity. The Bigfoot family, meanwhile, collected spruce tips, sweet grass and roots for their meals.

The lumberman was given reasonable freedom of the valley in which he was held, although always followed by at least two of the creatures. But eventually, fearing that he had been kidnapped as a possible husband for the female child, he took the opportunity to escape. He fed the largest (8 ft tall) Bigfoot some snuff and, while the creature rushed to bury his face in a stream, Ostman fled.

Reports of man-like beasts on the North American continent go back as far as the early 1800s. Indians told settlers stories about the wild, hairy creatures of the forests. They described them as being about 8 ft tall, with a broad chest and shoulders but virtually no neck.

But it was not until the early years of the nineteenth century that the first European, explorer David Thomas, discovered evidence of the strange animal - in the shape of footprints at least 14 in long, near Jasper, Alberta.

**Above:** *An expedition's tent on a glacier beneath the peak of Everest. One of the mountain's challengers was the first European to see a Yeti, in 1921.*

**Above:** *Edmund Hillary and Sherpa Tenzing, the conquerors of Everest, photographed returning in triumph in July 1953. Hillary found footprints but remained sceptical about the yeti.*

He had been held captive for an entire week but, fearing ridicule, did not tell his story for some time. And when he did, it seemed incredible...except for the many later pieces of evidence which backed his descriptions of the Bigfeet.

---

Lumberman Albert Ostman was carried by a giant male Bigfoot for over three hours until it reached its lair

---

At Mica Mountain, British Columbia in 1955 occurred one of the clearest sightings so far of a Bigfoot. It was made by William Roe, who was cunningly hidden in a bush when a female Bigfoot, standing about 6 ft tall, approached.

The massive creature, weighing around 300 lb, was unaware that she was being watched. When she got to within 20 feet of Roe she actually squatted by the bush in which he was hiding. This enabled Roe to make a thorough study.

He noted the shape of her head, what kind of face and hair she had, a description of her body and the way she walked. So extraordinary was the Bigfoot that Roe fleetingly wondered whether he had unwittingly stepped on to a film set.

His report of the encounter continued:

*Finally, the wild thing must have got my scent, for it looked directly at me through an opening in the bush. A look of amazement crossed its face. It looked so comical at that moment I had to grin. Still in a crouched position, it backed up three or four short steps, then straightened up to its full height and started to walk rapidly back the way it had come. For a moment it watched me over its shoulders as it went, not exactly afraid, but as though it wanted no contact with anything strange.*

Roe admitted that at the time he considered shooting this unique creature as proof of its existence. He even got to the point of raising his rifle and aiming. But Roe could not fire. 'Although I have called the creature "it", I feel now that it was a human being. And I knew I would never forgive myself if I killed it.'

### BREAKTHROUGH

The big breakthrough in the hunt for Bigfoot came on 20 October 1967. Roger Patterson, a former rodeo cowboy and rancher, was tracking the forests around Bluff Creek with an Indian friend, Bob Gimlin. They emerged into a clearing and, beside a creek, saw what they judged to be a female Bigfoot ambling along the bank. Patterson grabbed his 16mm movie camera and shot an amazing 29 feet of colour film as she loped across his field of vision. The pair also took casts of footprints left by the beast.

The shaky film was shown worldwide and most experts believed it to be genuine. But one copy was given to Bigfoot investigator Dr Napier, who believed that a hoax had been perpetrated. He wrote in his report: 'The upper part of the body bears some resemblance to an ape and the lower half is typically human. It is almost impossible to conceive that such structural hybrids could exist in nature. One half of the animal must be artificial.'

This leading expert on Bigfoot does have the final, convincing word on the mystery, however. He wrote: 'North American Bigfoot or Sasquatch has a lot going for it. Too many claim to have seen it, or at least to have seen footprints, to dismiss its reality out of hand.'